THE RAMBLING STORY
OF A DREAM

The Rambling Story of a Dream

THE AUTOBIOGRAPHY OF THE BUDDHIST MONK
Ven. Jianyue Duti
The Old Man Who Sees the Moon

Translated, edited, and researched by
Lynne Mallinson

Shaggy Yak Press

The Rambling Story of a Dream: The autobiography of the Buddhist monk Ven. Jianyue Duti, The Old Man Who Sees the Moon
Author: Ven. Jianyue Duti
Translated, edited, and researched by Lynne Mallinson

Copyright © 2024 by Lynne Mallinson

All rights reserved. This book or any portion thereof may not be reproduced or used in any manner whatsoever without the express written permission of the author, except for the use of brief quotations in a book review.

Printed in the United States of America

Luminare Press
442 Charnelton St.
Eugene, OR 97401
www.luminarepress.com

LCCN: 2024920119
ISBN: 979-8-88679-698-8

———◆———

The cover and title page graphics are based upon woodcuts from the eighteenth-century Baohua Shan Gazetteer.

Liu, Mingfang. *Baohua shan zhi*. 1784. Accessed on Internet Archive (27 June 2024). Contributed by: Cheng Yu Tung East Asian Library (University of Toronto), pp. 39–61. https://ia902906.us.archive.org/4/items/baohuashanzhi01lium/baohuashanzhi01lium.pdf

Table of Contents

Translator's Introduction . . . . *xiii*
Foreword by Vinaya Master Hongyi 1

PART ONE

1. What prompted me to write this memoir 7
2. An account of my early years 7
3. Living in the Xiao garden as the Daoist monk Huanji 9
4. Inspired by a Dream 12
5. Soliciting food donations for the monks and succouring the poor at the Sanying Dharma Assembly . . 14
6. Using my innate understanding of Buddhist principles to inculcate the Way 17
7. The Jianchuan Red Cliff Studio 19
8. The old monk of Xi Mountain 20
9. On Mount Jizu 22
10. Begging at Luoma 24
11. Receiving the tonsure at Fang'guang 25
12. I am requested to turn the Dharma Wheel 28
13. A Dharma talk at Qiyun Temple 29
14. Responding to questions concerning the Dharma at Lijiang 30
15. Invoking the purity rules for the first time 31
16. I first find out about the Vinaya 33
17. Setting off on foot in search of a Vinaya master 36
18. A farewell salute to ancestral tombs 37
19. Setting deep emotions aside and cutting off family ties . . 38
20. Crossing through the Biji and Jinma mountain passes . . 39
21. We purchase an arhat lantern 41
22. We travel through Guansuoling and cross the Pan River . . 42

23.	On the road to Anzhuangwei	44
24.	I copy a sūtra commentary at the Zhishui hermitage.	45
25.	Attending a seminar on the Śūraṅgama Sūtra at the Liangjia hermitage	48
26.	I need formal equipment to enter the lecture hall.	49
27.	Paying a visit to Grandmaster Zhuanyu	54
28.	Pheasant Lake	55
29.	Taking an alternate route to Jiangxi	56
30.	Visiting Lushan and paying our respects at the Donglin monastic community	58
31.	We travel to Jiujiang prefecture and pay our respects at monasteries founded by Chan patriarchs.	61
32.	At Taiping prefecture	64
33.	We reach Nanjing.	65
34.	If you aren't part of the saṃgha, you are not welcome in our midst.	66
35.	Monastic deportment	68
36.	Two people cannot register together.	69
37.	I ascend Baohua Mountain.	70
38.	A man of character does not partake of food of questionable provenance.	71
39.	Begging for ordination at Gulin hermitage	76
40.	On the road to Wutai Mountain	78
41.	Paying our respects to the elderly Monk Sanmei	79
42.	Sūtra-reading by lamplight	80
43.	My first time mounting the lecture podium	82
44.	Going to Beijing.	84
45.	We arrive in Baoding.	85
46.	I change my Buddhist name to Jianyue.	86
47.	We encounter an elderly monk on the road to Nangong county.	88
48.	Master Pingsu	89

49. Travelling from Danyang to the Haichao hermitage 91
50. Preceptor Xunliu 92
51. I repeatedly give up my seating space to others. 93
52. Memorizing the Vinaya 94
53. Taking turns lecturing on the Brahmā's Net Sūtra . . . 96
54. Subduing demonic obstructions 98
55. Painting a picture as a birthday gift for Sanmei 101
56. I do not change my Dharma name. 103
57. I am nominated to act as Preceptor Xun's replacement. My fellow Haichao ordinands' capable work generates an outstanding ordination. I learn the Vinaya by dint of bodhisattva insight. 104
58. I refuse a robe donated by my grateful class of novices. . . . 108

PART TWO

59. Master Xun requests that the Monk Sanmei bequeath the kāṣāya of Princess Rongchang to me. 113
60. Holding an ordination at the Bao'en Temple in Nanjing 116
61. I assign spaces to ordinands and exhort them to maintain proper comportment. 117
62. I act as one of the witnessing ācāryas at the ordination ceremony. 119
63. Harsh disciplinary measures are taken against delinquent monks. The ordination ceremony tallies perfectly with the dream that I had when I first went forth as a renunciate. 120
64. We escort Master Xun's remains to their final resting place. 121
65. Baohua Monastery. 122
66. Sanmei is formally requested to stay at Baohua as a permanent resident. 124

67. The Monk Sanmei takes over the command of Baohua Mountain. I am requested to act as the instruction master, as well as the prior, but I stipulate that four conditions be met before I accept the two positions. 126
68. Chengzhuo comes to the mountain to receive the precepts. 128
69. Great authority utilizes expedient means to bring me back to Baohua. 129
70. The pennant of Buddhism is erected on Mount Baohua. 131
71. Repositioning the temple by the labor of my own hands 132
72. I flee Mount Baohua. 134
73. Back to Baohua 137
74. I substitute for the Monk at the Guanyin hermitage. . . . 138
75. Mustering contributions 139
76. The collapse of the Ming dynasty in 1644 141
77. Strictly enforcing Buddhist regulations 141
78. I plan to have a stūpa erected in recognition of the Monk's benevolence. 142
79. Sanmei is taken ill and returns to Baohua. 144
80. Erecting a stūpa and deciding on a suitable location . . . 146
81. Sanmei confers the purple robe and Prātimokṣa upon me. 148
82. Circumstances spur me on to a higher level of spiritual attainment. 151
83. The prohibition of private cooking stoves 159
84. I insist upon strict adherence to Buddhist regulations. . . . 161
85. I chant the boundaries to establish a territory. We hold an ordination with three people on the platform at once. 163
86. I purchase a field in order to dispel murderous rancour. . . . 164
87. Bannermen set their horses loose in the fields and incite the peasants to revolt. 165

88. A retreat kept in strict purity ... 166
89. To avert calamity, we snare a rebel collaborator. ... 167
90. We demolish temple buildings. Master Yuanyun composes a commemorative poem. ... 172
91. One meal brings about the monastery's downfall. ... 174
92. Qing troops close in on Baohua. ... 175
93. Daily spiritual practice brings us strength in adversity. ... 178
94. In the face of adversity, I don't relinquish monastic deportment. ... 179
95. A righteous person does not utter falsehoods. ... 182
96. Walking at a steady pace, maintaining an impassive countenance ... 184
97. Black bannermen are replaced by a squad of green bannermen. ... 186
98. Those who keep the precepts do not use weapons. We endure hunger together, and when food is available, we share it equally amongst ourselves. ... 187
99. The assembly elects me as their abbot. Confiscated temple property is restored. Three Qing officials become Dharma protectors. ... 188
100. Way-follower Chen and Master Xiang ... 190
101. Interrogating a traitor ... 192
102. A lapse of temple discipline. We start building a wooden ordination platform for transmitting the complete precepts. ... 193
103. A longevity retreat assembly ... 195
104. My residence on the mountain inspires the local people. ... 198
105. Back at Baohua, I rectify lax management and strengthen monastic discipline. ... 200
106. We reduce temple rations in order to feed our starving neighbors. Supplicants chant the Buddha's name and cultivate blessings. ... 202

107. Visiting bhikṣuṇīs do not bow to the male saṃgha. I compile a guide entitled "Admonishing Bhikṣuṇīs on Proper Deportment and Discipline." 203
108. I undergo a three-month-long pratyutpanna-samādhi retreat twice. 207
109. I compose a Vinaya compendium as a guide for countless future generations of aspirants. 208

Appendices 211
Bibliography 233

Translator's Introduction

Ever since this seventeenth-century autobiography was composed, Chinese Buddhists have been deeply moved and inspired by Jianyue Laoren's[1] account of his life and times. The forward to the 1994 edition of this text, which was written in 1934 by Venerable Hongyi, amply attests to the reverence with which it has been received by Buddhist readers. *The Rambling Story of a Dream* is found in Chinese monastic libraries amidst a profusion of Indian scriptures and intricate commentaries.

Jianyue (1601–1679) was born in Yun'nan during the latter years of the Ming dynasty. He and his siblings lost their parents at an early age and were subsequently raised by their father's elder brother. An adventurous youth, Jianyue delighted in travel and was a convivial companion; however, his uncle's sudden death jolted him out of his lighthearted ways. He resolved to devote his life henceforth to spiritual practice in order to repay his uncle and parents for their care and protection. Indeed, filial piety and gratitude are oft-reiterated themes in this narrative. Jianyue's first venture into asceticism led him to Daoism, until a momentous dream redirected his intention to Buddhism. Part One of this autobiography recounts his sojourn through China in

---

1. "The Old Man Who Sees the Moon"

quest of Buddhist ordination, while Part Two chronicles Jianyue's equally arduous life as a prominent monk, and later, as the abbot of Baohua Monastery.

The narrative takes place during the Ming-Qing transition era. As Chinese culture and politics were being reshaped under succeeding dynasties and imperial reigns, the fortunes of Buddhism and Buddhist monasticism in China fluctuated substantially. For over a millenium, Buddhism had held a prominent place in Chinese society. Tibetan Buddhism was the Mongol Yuan dynasty's (1271–1368) official state religion. Zhu Yuanzhang (1328–1398), the founder of the Ming dynasty,[2] had lived in a Buddhist monastery as a youth. Buddhist monastics taught the future emperor to read and write, while his direct experience of temple life gave him a pragmatic understanding of the political and social ramifications of temple affairs. He realized that monastic autonomy would be a hindrance to his consolidation of power; on the other hand, he knew that Buddhist temples were also a potential revenue source.

Thus, officially recognizing Buddhism as one of the Three Teachings,[3] the Hongwu Emperor (r. 1521–1564) instituted tight controls over Buddhist monastic activities. Ordinations, exams, passports, monies, and publications were only a few aspects of monastic life that were subject to tight governmental control. Subsequently, this policy was continued under a series of emperors, until the Jiajing Emperor (r. 1368–1398)[4] suspended Buddhist ordinations and allowed the stringent regulation system to lapse. Official ordination platforms in

---

2. Ming Dynasty (1368–1644)

3. i.e., Confucianism, Daoism, and Buddhism

4. The Jiajing ("Splendid Tranquility") Emperor favored Daoism, which offered longevity potions to support his palace debauchery.

Translator's Introduction

Beijing and Nanjing were closed down in 1526.

Jianyue's narrative unfolds at a time when the practice of precept transmission had waned. Opportunities to receive the precepts were rare, and the Vinaya tradition had lapsed into obscurity. Only when he overheard a conversation between his Buddhist master and some temple visitors did Jianyue discover that he was not an "official" monk: he had never received the full precepts. He set off at once on a quest to receive final ordination under the ministrations of Sanmei Jiguang, the sole remaining exponent of the Vinaya tradition. Jianyue's lengthy and toilsome journey was further complicated by the country's state of political turbulence at a time when Ming authority was disintegrating and the Manchu Qing empire was gaining momentum.

After an arduous journey through China, Jianyue was finally ordained by Sanmei Jiguang (1580–1645). Sanmei had been ordained by Guxin Ruxin (1541–1616), who had never received a proper ordination but became recognized as a Vinaya master. Due to Guxin Ruxin's widespread influence and innovative ordination procedures,[5] the Wanli Emperor (r. 1572–1620) once again sanctioned Buddhist ordinations. In his autobiography, Jianyue recounts his extensive travels to organize and lead massive ordination assemblies as Sanmei's attendant.

———◆———

Jianyue's autobiography will be of interest to religious adherents and the general reader alike, as well as to stu-

---

5. Guxin Ruxin initiated triple-platform ordinations that allowed novice initiation, full ordination, and bodhisattva ordination to be conducted in the same place within short intervals of time.

dents of Chinese Buddhism, history, and theology. It is an adventure story that winds its way through hazards, safe havens, and scores of curious incidents. Along his path, Jianyue encounters an array of striking characters: scholars, artists, generals, members of the imperial court, gentry, villagers, and rascals. This book is a travelogue full of local color that offers a first-hand glimpse into a tumultuous era of political unrest.

This travel record also hints at an ideological trend that has been noted by contemporary historians. In Jianyue's era, the Chinese were redefining their homeland in emulation of India's ancient marvels and lore. Rather than accept their country's marginalization as a "borderland" lying outside the marvelous land in which the Buddhist tradition was born, literati and religious circles were endeavoring to redefine and enrich China's domestic landscape. Holy mountains were identified, while other geographical features were invested with ancient legends and supernatural beings. In this way, China could once again claim to be the Middle Kingdom, the center of the world. Indeed, the Vinaya tradition that Jianyue promoted had been reignited by Guxin Ruxin, whose authority was validated by his vision of the Indian bodhisattva Mañjuśrī on Mount Wutai.

But the book's academic and historical value is only of secondary importance in comparison with the example set by this scruffy, irascible monk. Jianyue remains steadfastly immune to both good fortune and bad: honor, wealth, and power hold as little grip on him as do poverty, hunger, extreme weather conditions, and the horrors of war. Regardless of passing circumstances, he still adheres rigorously to the Buddhist Dharma; he never becomes cynical and never condones his fellow Buddhists' lax compromises.

Translator's Introduction

Perhaps modern readers will find clarity and inspiration in Jianyue's stark integrity.

The present translation was originally intended to level the text into a flat narrative with as few explanatory notes as possible, thus paving a smooth road for the modern reader to tread. Even with the kindest of intentions, though, it soon became clear that the translation would be flimsy without a solid foundation of footnotes. In his autobiography, Jianyue is addressing his fellow monastics, who are naturally familiar with Buddhist doctrine and practices and have experienced the vicissitudes of war and dynastic change. The cities, villages, waterways, mountains, and farmers' fields depicted in Jianyue's autobiography would have been easily envisioned by his first readers. In order to accommodate present-day readers, historical circumstances and curious details are explained in the footnotes and appendices, along with marginal comments written by Ven. Hongyi. Every person and Buddhist practice center that appears in this narrative has a tale to tell, and I have endeavored to sketch in some of these subplots whenever possible.

Numerous details remain to be clarified. For example, it would be satisfying to pinpoint the exact function of each "hermitage" (*an*) in which Jinayue lodged. The Chinese character *an* that appears frequently in the text can be construed as a convent, a small temple, or a rustic retreat. Imperial gazetteers might furnish more precise information, but such invaluable research tools were not available for the present translation. Secondly, the presence of women in this travelogue remains largely unstated due to the ubiquitous

The Rambling Story of a Dream

usage of the male third-person pronoun in the Chinese language prior to the 1919 May Fourth Movement. Women only appear definitively when a nun attempts to lead Sanmei to safety and when "unruly" nuns visit Baohua to study. If the opportunity arises for a future edition, more such details will be delved into, some of my abundant errors will be cleared up, and additional features like maps will be drawn.

Much of this translation was completed during the recent pandemic with the aid of online reference materials. So many websites had to be sifted through and then weighed against countless others that a full bibliography would be unwieldy and impossible to compile. Honorable mention must be given to The Digital Dictionary of Buddhism, edited by Charles Muller, which has often filled in gaps in my knowledge or, at least, indicated in which direction answers were to be found. A few online authors provided me with valuable insight into the era's cultural texture. To name only two instances, an article by H. Zurndorfer filled me in on Ming- and Qing-dynasty social turbulence, while Beata Grant's research on seventeenth-century female Chan masters alerted me to the sizeable presence of women living in monastic communities and private retreats during that time period. My deepest gratitude goes to the late Johannes Prip-Møller and Holmes Welch, both of whose invaluable research has enhanced my understanding considerably. Although not contemporaneous with this narrative, the information that they collected still provides a detailed image of monastic life.

The appendices consist of a desultory attempt at a glossary, some information on the bureaucratic hierarchy that once existed in large Buddhist monasteries, and a brief history of Baohua Monastery.

Translator's Introduction

My thanks go to the University of Oregon, Eugene, which extends a cordial welcome to ripe-aged community members. Much of this translation was typed at the U of O Knight Library.

Finally, I would like to thank Bhikṣuṇī Jendy Shih of the American Evergreen Buddhist Association in Kirkland, Washington, who launched me on this impossible project, provided two published editions of the text, and contributed funding for this book's publication.

Foreword by Vinaya Master Hongyi

I came across this volume while browsing through a Buddhist monastery's book catalogue. There, an entry entitled *The Rambling Story of a Dream* caught my eye. I got the impression that it was a Buddhist text written by a modern author whose intention it was to offer guidance and advice to lay readers. I borrowed a copy.

Only when I began reading it did I learn that it was the autobiographical account of the Ming-dynasty Jianyue Laoren of Baohua Monastery, in which he recounts his experiences as a wandering pilgrim. I was overjoyed, profoundly aware of the book's incomparable preciousness. I read it over and over again, even forgetting to eat. I was stunned—so deeply moved that I broke into tears again and again.

In order to make Venerable Jianyue's autobiography more accessible for modern readers, I immediately set to work on a new edition and provided supplementary reference materials. The original text was composed as a single uninterrupted narrative. I divided the story into sections, added marginal comments and elucidations, and drew a map showing the route that Jianyue traversed on his travels.[6] I hope that my edited version and addenda

---

6. This map has since been lost.

will smooth the way for future textual research and make it easily comprehensible for modern readers.

Throughout his life, both when dealing with people and carrying out his duties, Venerable Jianyue[7] consistently maintained a stately, dignified demeanor and never showed kindness. One might say that he was overly stern, that he distanced himself from human relationships and feelings. But in these latter-day times when the Buddhist Dharma has fallen into decay, "admirable friendships"[8] that are formed by Buddhist practitioners may well be lacking in true wisdom and compassion. Whether within a monastery or between monastics and lay-persons, easy-going friendship is prone to contamination by popular vulgarity. Some claim that such *camaraderie* is an expedient means of inculcating the Dharma, that they are going along with common social customs out of compassion. But perhaps that's only an excuse to justify their own slackness.

The words and deeds of the venerable monk whose autobiography appears in this book are the perfect antidote to such hypocrisy. There is a Confucian saying: "Upon hearing of Boyi's[9] outstanding virtue, even an avaricious person will become honorable, and a coward, resolute." In my opinion, this quote squarely applies to Venerable Jianyue.

---

7. The deeds and achievements of Jianyue (1601–1679) are also recorded in the "Baohua Mountain Gazetteer" and the *Record of Pure-Land Sages*.

8. *Kalyāṇa-mitratā* [Skt.] refers to spiritual friendship among seekers of the Way. (*shanzhishi* [Ch.])

9. Boyi was renowned for his rigorous Confucian virtue.

Foreword by Vinaya Master Hongyi

By August 10th, 1934, I had completed a close study of the text and recited it aloud from cover to cover. By the 25th, I had finished taking notes on its contents. At the time, I was living at the Jin River hermitage.[10]

By September 5th, when I had nearly completed and corrected a timeline of the main events in Jianyue's life, I was also editing *The Rambling Story of a Dream*. I revised and enhanced the original text, adding punctuation, chapter divisions, and my own comments. Finally, I wrote this forward. On September 13th, I finished composing a glossary of terms in the order of their appearance in the text.

Lying in bed, I reflected upon the events of Jianyue Laoren's life and vowed to travel to Baohua Mountain to venerate his stūpa. Tears poured down uncontrollably from my eyes. I felt deeply grieved by the waning and passing away of the Buddhist Vinaya tradition. The pain of this realization pierced me to the bottom of my heart.

—Hongyi at the Jin River Hermitage
of the South Putuo Temple

---

10. That year, from spring until autumn, Ven. Hong Yi was living on the back mountain of the South Putuo Temple in the *Tuṣita* compound, which he called the Jin River hermitage.

Part One

What prompted me to write this memoir

In the winter of the year 1674, during the Kangxi[11] imperial reign,[12] Master Liyan and the other *ācāryas*,[13] as well as our group leaders and temple officials,[14] respectfully asked me for an account of my pilgrimages, visits to eminent monks, and other noteworthy experiences, in order to inspire future generations of monastics. Thus, I have taken up "*Guanchengzi*,"[15] my trusty brush, to recount the events of my life straightforwardly, rambling on from beginning to end without adding any literary embellishment.

An account of my early years

I was born into the Xu family in Yun'nan province's Chuxiong prefecture. When I was fourteen years of age and my two

---

11. The Qing-dynasty Kangxi Emperor (r. 1661–1722) was one of China's greatest rulers.

12. Jianyue was seventy-three when he wrote this memoir.

13. *ācārya* [Skt.]: preceptor

14. *zhishi*: A fuller elucidation of temple officers is provided in the appendix.

15. The term first appears in the Tang-dynasty essay *Maoying zhuan* by Han Yu (768–824 CE), one of China's greatest prose masters. The essay features a laborious allegory in which the protagonist Maoying is also a writing brush. Other characters appear as personifications of ink sticks, mulberry paper, and inkstones. The appellation "Guan Chengzi" (Tube City) alludes to the bamboo tube of a writing brush.

See William H. Nienhauser, Jr., "An Allegorical Reading of Han Yü's *Mao-Ying Chuan*" (Biography of Fur Point),

Oriens Extremus, Vol. 23, No. 2 (1976), pp. 153–174. https://www.jstor.org/stable/43382488

younger brothers were both very young, my father died and my mother passed away soon afterwards. The three of us were left miserably alone, with no one to take care of us. My father's elder brother was childless and getting on in years; hence, he was doubly affectionate towards us and willingly became our benefactor and teacher. Around that time, I painted a picture of Guanyin Bodhisattva, which impressed people so much that they called me "Little Wu Daozi."[16]

I loved to wander to far places and see the world—I never stopped walking. In 1626, the sixth year of the Tianqi reign,[17] I was twenty-five years old. That year, I heard about the Golden Sands River located on the border of Dali prefecture and northern Shengzhou. It was said that those who lived along the river made their living by panning for gold. My curiosity quickened, I invited a few comrades to accompany me on a five hundred *li* [18] walking trip to see if this story were true. When we got there, we verified its accuracy: the Earth had bestowed its bounty upon these people. Gold-panning was really their livelihood!

I also heard about another wonder in Heqing prefecture. It was said that the mountains there tower aloft straight and tall as walls, damming the river and making the roads hazardous for travellers. In ancient times, there was a snake goblin who dreamt of transforming the river into an ocean. In the southeastern section, the land lies low and hollow. That area is called Dianwei. When the river flows into this place, it is obstructed, accumulates in a deep pool, and gradually

---

16. Wu Daozi (685–758) was a renowned Tang-dynasty painter.

17. The Tianqi Emperor (r. 1620–1627) was the 16th Ming ruler.

18. Around 155 miles. One *li* equals approximately .5 kilometers or .31 miles. The *li* was never a centrally-defined unit, but rough conversions will be provided throughout this translation.

floods its banks. The divine Indian monk Venerable Magadha felt compassion for the beleaguered local inhabitants and decided to save them. He took up his tin-ringed staff[19] and used it to bore scores of holes that were over five *li* long[20] into the base of the mountain. In this way, he caused the pent-up waters to flow into Golden Sands River.

During my visit, I met the scholar Xiao Anchu of Langqiong county. In Chuxiong, he had once commissioned a portrait of Guanyin[21] from me. He was delighted to see me again and invited me to come to Langqiong county. Afterwards, Li Lian, Yang Shaoxian, and others came to visit us. Xiao Anchu and Yang Shaoxian were relatives. Both were from Jufu and owned famous gardens and country villas. Everybody got along splendidly, so I spent a year with them.

Living in the Xiao garden as the Daoist monk Huanji

I was twenty-seven years old in 1628, the first year of the Chongzhen[22] imperial reign. Early in the twelfth lunar month of that year, some good friends and I were taking a leisurely stroll through a plum garden that was about twenty *li* [23] from Langqiong county. Xiao Anchu had a scholarly retreat there abutting Shibao Mountain. He owned over an acre of property on which he had planted hundreds of pear trees; throughout the year, one could enjoy every kind of flower and plant. Everyone was

---

19. *khakkara* [Skt.]: a staff with metal rings attached to the top that is traditionally carried by Buddhist monks

20. several miles in length

21. Guanyin: Avalokiteśvara [Skt.]

22. The Chongzhen Emperor (r. 1627–1644) was the last Ming-dynasty ruler.

23. approximately seven miles

drinking, conversing, and laughing gaily. Just when our outing was at its most convivial, I received a letter from my hometown: my uncle had been missing me ever since I left and had been hoping for my return. He passed away not long after reaching his seventieth year, unable to see me one last time. The news shocked me into sobriety; broken-hearted, I cried bitterly. Previously, I had never believed in Buddhism or Daoism, but now, I suddenly formed the intention of becoming a monk.

I told my friends, "My behavior has been deeply unfilial. I owe a great debt to my mother, my father, and my uncle for the grace that they have bestowed upon me. I must atone for my transgressions. Here and now, I vow to go forth and become an ascetic, do repentance for my sins, and repay the loving-kindness bestowed upon me by my benefactors. From this moment on, we must part ways forever, never again to meet."

Hearing these words, my comrades all stared at me wide-eyed, thinking that I had gone mad.

Xiao Anchu protested, "You can't go a single day without drinking wine: how can you possibly become a renunciate and follow a strict vegetarian diet? If you really want to renounce the secular world, there's no need to go anywhere else—I'll give you this entire garden as a charitable donation. You can live here and do spiritual practice."

Yang Shaoxian said, "Since Brother Xiao has decided to donate his residence, I'll take care of all your daily needs and donate my boy servant to do your bidding and run errands."

To this, I responded, "How fortunate I am that you gentlemen will take care of my needs as a renunciate. Clearly, we are linked by many lifetimes of excellent karma. By furnishing food and drink, clothing, bedding, and medicine,[24] you will amply manifest our profound karmic ties. But I entreat you never to allow meat or wine to be brought into this villa. Any amount of rice and firewood will be fine. You can provide vegetarian meals, anything that is appropriate for the life of an itinerant ascetic."

Needing no strenuous persuasion, my friends joyfully promised to comply with these requests.

There happened to be a Daoist temple located about twenty *li* from the garden, so I went there to pay my respects. I told the residents of my intention to renounce secular life. One elderly priest wanted to lure me into becoming his disciple. I noticed that his bearing lacked dignity and correctness; moreover, his conversation was senseless and unreasonable. Hedging, I asked him to allow me to go back home and think it over, then return with an answer. On his table lay a Daoist text entitled *The Collected Scriptures Recounting the Deeds of the Jade Emperor*.[25] I wanted to take it home and read it.

When I asked to borrow it, he replied, "You aren't a Daoist priest, so you are not entitled to make such a request!"

I immediately took off my lay clothing and put on the Daoist robe that he provided.

Thereupon, he told me, "Since you're really entering the priesthood, you are now authorized to request the Jade Emperor Classic."

I took the volume back to the Xiao garden and placed it ceremoniously on my desk. Kneeling on the floor, I made a solemn prostration, bringing my forehead to the ground with my hands palm-upwards. Then, I changed my name

---

24. the four material needs of a monk

25. The *Gaoshang yuhuang benxing jijing*, attributed to the Jade Emperor, is included in the Daoist Canon.

The Rambling Story of a Dream

to Zhenyuan (Primary Truth) and assumed the courtesy name Huanji (Return to the Ultimate).

Inspired by a Dream

On the thirtieth day of the twelfth lunar month, I wrote a Jade Emperor spirit tablet[26] and set offerings before it. Intoning the god's name with great sincerity, I carried out a religious ceremony. By the middle of the night, I was exhausted and slumped senseless to the ground, sound asleep.

Dreaming, I beheld the boundless clear blue sky with the red sun beaming down from on high. I came upon a large temple. Its halls and platforms were towering and spacious. A red wall encircled the compound, along with a row of pines and cedars. In the middle, there was a doorway. Within, I could see some monks: all had shaven heads and wore monastic robes.[27] I was delighted and wanted to enter, but the doorsill was too high for me to leap over. I exerted myself to the utmost and tried repeatedly to cross over it.

Suddenly, I was on the other side. As soon as I had entered the monastery grounds, I felt that I was no longer a Daoist—I now looked like a Buddhist monk. Then, I noticed that the monks were all standing around a high platform on which an elderly monk clad in a red robe presided as the head seat.[28] Smiling broadly, he beckoned to me. I pushed through the assembly of monks and approached him.

---

26. Spirit tablets are usually done on red paper with brush calligraphy to honor deities or ancestors.

27. *kāṣāya*: the robe traditionally worn by Buddhist monastics

28. *shangzuo* (rector)

Inspired by a Dream

The elderly monk picked up a book and handed it to me, saying, "Announce this to the monks."

I took the volume and stood beside the platform. As I read it, the monks all knelt on the floor and listened.

When I awoke, my body was soaked with sweat and I could no longer recall the contents of the book that I had been reading aloud.

"I'm not a Daoist after all," I reflected, "I'll have to become a Buddhist monk."

The rising sun ushered in the year 1629, the second Chongzhen regnal year; I was twenty-eight years old. From that time on, my daily practice was to kneel and recite the Jade Emperor Classic. Every three days, I performed a ceremony of repentance in which I expressed gratitude for the benevolence that I had received from others. This was my regular monastic practice. Every time I did a repentance ceremony, I remembered the past and prayed. Overcome with sorrow and sobbing bitterly, I would express my intention of repaying the grace that had been bestowed upon me.

When my former comrades came to visit the garden, which was now a temple, they saw that my previous vulgarity was entirely gone: I was genuinely devoting myself to spiritual practice without the slightest lapse into laziness. Seeing how I'd changed, everyone felt a surge of religious faith and had nothing but praise for my new life. Some of my friends vowed to become vegetarians, while others wanted to renounce the secular world and become monks. From that time on, everyone for miles around knew that a Daoist recluse named Huanji was staying at the Xiao family villa.

The Rambling Story of a Dream

Soliciting food donations for the monks and succouring the poor at the Sanying Dharma Assembly

Around eighty *li* [29] from the walls of Langqiong county was the town of Sanying. In this town was the Dajue (Great Enlightenment) Temple. In the spring of 1630,[30] there were plans to hold a Longhua[31] Buddhist assembly there. During the Lantern Festival,[32] I paid the temple a visit. It just so happened that the head monk Yun'guan[33] and everyone involved in planning the gathering were present in the main hall. After making obeisance to the Buddha with solemn reverence, I went and sat down in the dining hall. A white-haired lay Buddhist[34] wearing a square black Confucian hat came over to me, joining his palms ceremoniously to signify welcome. He inquired from whence I had come.

I replied, "I have come from Langqiong."

"Have you perchance met the Daoist Huanji who is staying at the Xiao family residence?" he inquired. "What Daoist recitations does he perform? How lofty is his spiritual practice?" the lay Buddhist pursued.

---

29. approximately twenty-five miles

30. the third Chongzhen regnal year

31. The future Buddha Maitreya will be enlightened under the Longhua tree, where he will teach the Dharma thrice; each time, multitudes of disciples will come to listen, many of whom will become enlightened arhats. In Maitreya's first teaching, he will address the spiritually gifted; the second teaching will be for those of middling attainments; and in his third teaching, he will bring salvation to those whose storehouse of merit is base and undeveloped.

Maitreya is revered by Mahayana Buddhists because he bestows universal salvation. By contrast, Hinayana Buddhists believe that enlightenment is the fruit of long and intense spiritual cultivation.

32. a festival marking the final day of the traditional Chinese New Year celebration

33. Cloudy Pass

34. *gṛhapati* [Skt.]: a householder, a lay patron of a Buddhist community

I replied, "I've gotten a glimpse of him, but all I know about him comes from hearsay, since no one is allowed to meet him. He's only pretending to practise self-cultivation; it's really all for show, bolstered by groundless rumors. It's just a cheat. Anyway, he's only been a renunciate for a short while, so how can he possibly have attained such lofty virtue or such an intense spiritual practice?"

At that, the elderly lay Buddhist gave me a black look and told me sternly, "Since you practise the Way, you should praise people of virtue. If you notice that someone has erred, then you should kindly overlook their failings. But with your evident jealousy of this Way-friend, you'll certainly never pass for a real spiritual practitioner!"

Just then, another lay Buddhist entered the room. He recognized me and gave me a happy salute.

Noticing this, the elderly lay Buddhist asked him, "Do you know this Daoist?"

"That's Master Huanji, who resides at the Xiao family villa!" he replied.

At that, the old man exclaimed, "I nearly let slip a golden opportunity!"

He immediately conveyed the news to the head monk and the meeting leaders. They all saluted me and greeted me cordially, and then implored me to act as one of the assembly heads at the main altar.

I protested, "A person authorized to preside on the Longhua platform should be deeply-versed in esoteric Buddhist philosophy and familiar with monastic practices. I only meditate and chant, I'm totally unqualified to assume a leadership role here."

They kept up their entreaties, which I met with three refusals. Finally, it was clear that everyone was determined to enlist me and would accept no refusal.

"In such a large Buddhist gathering," I countered, "the most important responsibility is soliciting alms to feed and shelter the *saṃgha*. Have you started preparing for this?"

The group leaders admitted that they hadn't gotten around to it.

I continued, "How can your assembly count as a grand gathering if vegetarian meals are not provided for the monks? I'll do my best to take care of that for you. First of all, it will enable the lay practitioners to keep the monastery atmosphere solemn and dignified; secondly, virtuous people of faith can be induced to gain merit by giving alms."

As soon as they heard my proposal, everyone was overjoyed. They bowed and thanked me.

The next day, I set off to visit the town's prominent citizens, hoping to persuade them to take the initiative and sponsor the Buddhist gathering. Someone told me that Town Magistrate Ai and Commander Lü were connected by marriage as father- and son-in-law. They were wealthy and charitable; moreover, they were close relatives of Xiao Anchu of Langqiong county. Clearly, they were outstanding candidates for my alms campaign. It seemed to me that my prospects of success were good, so I went first to pay my respects to the Lü family.

Upon reaching their front gates, I ran into a messenger who had been sent by Xiao Anchu to deliver gifts. I took advantage of the chance encounter and asked him to announce me when he entered the Lü residence. Thus, I obtained an invitation to enter. Dharma protector Ai also happened to be present. Although he had heard of me, he had never met me personally. I told him about the Buddhist assembly's need for financial support.

He replied, "How can they possibly initiate a Longhua Buddhist gathering without alms to feed the monks? Since Master Huanji is willing to take the matter in hand, this old fellow wishes to advocate for you."

He straightaway sent a messenger to invite the virtuous town residents and other benevolent people of faith to come together for a group discussion. Everyone was delighted to participate.

The next day, Ai and Lü, the two Dharma protectors, stood on my left and right sides. One held a blue parasol and the other a yellow one. I was between them, clad in my Daoist robes and wearing straw sandals, and the town elders and other people of good faith and charitable intentions accompanied us. Together, we visited every street and alleyway, large and small. Everyone exhorted their friends and family members to give alms to support the Buddhist monks. On that day, we received over three hundred silver *taels* and five hundred bushels[35] of rice.

Using my innate understanding of Buddhist principles to inculcate the Way

As soon as we returned to the temple, we engaged workmen to build scores of thatched cottages; additionally, we borrowed utensils and articles of daily use from everyone. Our only remaining problem was finding a suitable person to act as the kitchen supervisor.

That afternoon, an itinerant monk walked in. His appearance was quaint; his voice was gentle but powerful. We asked where he had come from. He told us that he had just made

---

35. bushels: One *dan* is defined as the amount that can be carried on a shoulder-pole.

The Rambling Story of a Dream

a pilgrimage to Jizu Mountain.[36] He was from Xundian prefecture; his Buddhist name was Chengzhuo.[37] I asked him to lend a hand and he assented right away. With the Way ever foremost in his mind, he worked hard day and night, never showing fatigue, always patient and courteous. Since we both cherished similar ideals, we became staunch Way-friends.

Every day, no fewer than a thousand itinerant Buddhist monks and Daoists came to the temple for religious observances and vegetarian meals; additionally, hundreds of orphans, widows, mendicants, and poor people visited daily. I urged everyone who came to the temple and donated alms to make reverence to the saṃgha and pray for good fortune. I also explained to them that according to the Buddhist worldview, some of the destitute temple visitors may well have been our parents or close relatives in previous lifetimes. Because they had neglected to make offerings to the Three Jewels of Buddhism—the Buddha, the Dharma, and the Saṃgha—and had never aided the poor and afflicted, they were now suffering the bitter fruits of their past failings.

"You and I," I opined, "are only common mortals: our fleshly eyes cannot peer into previous lifetimes to witness the intricate strands of dependent origination. We must subdue our toxic habits of arrogance and egotism and worship with deep respect."

Hearing these words, my listeners were convinced and heeded my counsel. They were from the Yun'nan area; since

---

36. Mount Kukkutapāda or Mount Gurupāda: Jizu (Chicken-foot) Mountain is named after an Indian holy mountain. Mount Jizu is a sacred mountain for Chinese Buddhists, Daoists, and local shamanistic cults.

37. Chengzhuo: 'Becoming Clumsy.' Master Hongyi remarks here (and I concur) that Chengzhuo is the most appealing figure in this narrative. Hongyi was so impressed by the itinerant monk's character and conduct that he circled every passage in which Chengzhuo appears.

ancient times, such words of guidance were a rarity in that part of China. I had never studied any scriptures—the teachings that I was able to inculcate arose spontaneously through my own innate understanding.[38]

When the gathering was drawing to a close, I heard the group leaders privately making plans to give me a gift as a reward for my help. The day before the Buddhist assembly was to end, I went secretly to Chengzhuo to say goodbye. Before the day dawned, I went quietly back to Langqiong.

The Jianchuan Red Cliff Studio

In the year 1631, the fourth Chongzhen regnal year, I was thirty years old. In the middle of the second lunar month, the brothers Li Junfu and Li Junbi were in Jianchuan. Both were well-known in the scholarly realm and had profound faith in the Three Jewels. We often got together. They had a literati retreat about thirty *li* from the city walls of Jianchuan in a remote, secluded area. It lay among ancient green pines and elegant red cliffs. They invited me there to pursue self-cultivation in this tranquil setting.

They were on the best of terms with Xiao Anchu, so they sent a messenger to deliver a letter to him explaining their intentions. At first, Anchu was hesitant about my departure. As a Way-friend, he was loth to part with me, but due to the Confucian code of friendship, he also felt obligated to accede to the wishes of the Li brothers. He was torn between these two conflicting considerations. I told him that Jianchuan wasn't really so far away; hence, it was better for him to accept the brothers' invitation and let me

---

38. i.e., karmic causation, *nidāna*

go. Thus, I took my leave of the Xiao family residence and went to the Li villa as requested.

I arrived on the fifteenth day of the third lunar month. In this new location, I continued my previous vegetarian regime and was ever more diligent[39] in pursuing my spiritual practice. Seeing my glad perseverance, the two Li brothers were moved to intensify their faith, and the elder brother vowed to practise vegetarianism for the rest of his life.

The old monk of Xi Mountain

At the beginning of the sixth lunar month, the weather was blazing hot. In order to cool off, I hiked up to the top of a red cliff. On the summit was an enormous boulder: I sat cross-legged upon it. Looking towards the west, my field of vision extended for about five miles into the distance.

Far away, hemmed in by mountains and luxuriant forests—could that be an ancient temple? I got up and walked in that direction. Up close, it turned out to be a thatched cottage. Through its half-closed bamboo door came the sound of a *muyu*[40] being struck and the murmur of sūtra chanting. I waited outside until the chanting was over and then entered. Within was an elderly monk of dignified demeanor.

I made obeisance, and he remarked, "You Yellow Hats[41] usually don't bow to Buddhist monks. Where have you come from? What are your formal and style names?"

"I am called Huanji; I live at the Xiao residence in Langqiong. Right now, I am staying at the Red Cliff Studio."

Hearing this, he joined his hands in salute. "I've heard

---

39. Vīrya [Skt.]: engaging in wholesome activities with energy and enthusiasm
40. A 'wooden fish' that is tapped during Buddhist ceremonies
41. A synechdoche signifying Daoist priests, who wear yellow hats.

that Master Huanji attended the Longhua assembly at Sanying, where he fed the monks and aided the poor without discriminating between wealthy and poor households; moreover, he is skillful at giving spiritual guidance to almsgivers and worshippers. He has realized the emptiness[42] of the self."

The monk continued, "Who is your teacher? Which sūtras have you studied? What learning has enabled you to do such prodigious Buddhist work?"

I answered, "I have no teacher, nor have I read any Buddhist sūtras or learnt any of the Buddha's teachings. Both my understanding of Buddhism and everything that I've done have come from personal intuition."

Amazed, he declared, "Your actions show the compassion of a bodhisattva; you have cultivated the spiritual faculty of wisdom. Make haste and become the disciple of a brilliant, distinguished master; shave your head and become a Buddhist monk. Thus, you can promote the Buddhist teachings and provide transformative guidance to all sentient beings."

The elderly sage continued, "It is my regular practice to recite the Flower Garland Sūtra.[43] You can borrow it if you like. When you read it, you must kneel respectfully. Some of the basic principles of Buddhism and Daoism are superficial, while others are profound, but a bodhisattva's vow of compassion and strict observance of the Buddhist precepts are boundless and limitless. Since you've developed bodhicitta[44] naturally, you don't require the instruction of others."

---

42. *śūnyatā* [Skt.]: the Buddhist notion that all things are void of intrinsic existence and nature

43. *Mahāvaipulya Buddhāvataṃsaka Sūtra*

44. The mind of enlightenment that strives toward awakening and compassion for the benefit all sentient beings

The Rambling Story of a Dream

Hearing his words, I bowed and thanked the monk for his guidance, then borrowed the Flower Garden Sūtra and returned to Red Cliff. There, I burned incense, knelt down, and read the first chapter in its entirety—"The Wondrous Adornments of the Rulers of the World." As I read, I remembered the dream that I had had when I first renounced the world. All of a sudden, I stood up, determined to take the tonsure and don Buddhist robes.[45]

On Mount Jizu

At the end of the seventh lunar month, Miaozong, the abbot of a large temple in Langqiong county, paid me a visit. He brought me a letter from Xiao Anchu and invited me to join him on a pilgrimage to Mount Jizu. Their timing was perfect, it was just what I had been waiting for. I immediately took leave of the two Li brothers and accompanied Miaozong on his trip to meet Anchu. We arrived on the fifteenth day of the eighth lunar month and spent the night at the Jiguang[46] Temple.

We were told that Master Wuming[47] lived in the mountains there; we also heard about the two retired abbots Baiyun[48] and Dali,[49] who lived on Lion Peak and devoted themselves to refined spiritual practice in order to be reborn in the Pure Land. In thirty years, they had never once come down from their hermitage.

I spent eighteen days with Miaozong and Anchu roaming in the mountains. We passed through pine forests, rambled

---

45. *kāṣāya*
46. Quiet Light
47. Without Brightness (intelligence)
48. White Cloud
49. Great Force

On Mount Jizu

along woodland streams and pathways, descended into mountain valleys, and climbed steep cliffs.

Finally, we reached the hermitage. We made obeisance to the venerable monks and entreated them to tonsure me as a Buddhist monk. Retired abbot Dali made a thorough examination of my background and motivation for seeking ordination. Finally, out of deep compassion, my request was granted: he told me to prepare my robe and bowl.

At this, Anchu said, "Since you have graciously accepted Huanji, please allow me, your disciple, to supply his robes, alms bowl, vegetarian meal offering, and all of his other equipment."

The former abbot Baiyun observed, "This person will accomplish great deeds and achieve outstanding realization. His ordination cannot be done carelessly and hastily. If receiving the Buddhist precepts is too easy, the ordinand will not be steadfast in upholding his vows. In order to subdue his self-centered arrogance and test the firmness of his intentions, this ordinand should go from door-to-door begging. Once he has obtained his robe and bowl by begging, he can come back here to be tonsured."

I inwardly marveled at their benevolent wisdom: one master had compassionately accepted my request, while the other wished to subdue my conceited pride. I felt awe and veneration for these spiritual friends. There was such a marked difference between Buddhism and Daoism. Buddhism was prudent and exacting, whereas Daoism seemed loose and unregulated.

Knowing in my heart that circumstances were still unripe for my ordination, I held back my tears and told them, "I will follow your instructions faithfully, yet since I have come all this way through the mountains to reach

The Rambling Story of a Dream

your hermitage, it seems a pity to go back empty-handed. I entreat you venerable Monks[50] to show compassion and give me a Dharma name. Although my head is still unshaven, I can temporarily cherish this monastic identity in my heart."

Hearing my entreaty, the retired abbot Dali broke into a smile. He gave me the Dharma name Shuqiong.

Begging at Luoma

I bowed and went outside, mentally formulating a step-by-step plan for carrying out the Monks' instructions.

As I cudgeled my brain indecisively, a monk named Yuefeng[51] came over and inquired, "Daoist, what are you thinking about?"

I replied, "I'm trying to figure out where to go begging for monastic robes and an alms bowl, but I'm unfamiliar with this area."

He offered a suggestion: "If you start from Langqiong and travel two hundred *li* [52] through the Phoenix-Tail Mountains, you will come to a place called Luomajing. It is a salt-producing town. Twenty or thirty thousand families reside there; the inhabitants are wealthy and benevolent. I'm from Luomajing.

"As it happens," he continued, "I'll be going there to pay my respects to my Buddhist master in a few days. It seems that you've never been there before, so you're welcome to come along with me."

At the end of the ninth lunar month, I left Jizu with Yuefeng, heading towards Phoenix-Tail. It took us over half

---

50. Monk (*heshang*) is the title for an abbot. It is capitalized in this translation.
51. Moon Peak
52. around 62 miles

Receiving the tonsure

a month to reach Luomajing. There, we stayed at the Xishan Fang'guang Temple.[53] Wuzong, the head monk, received us with delighted cordiality: his warm welcome was quite unlike the aloof reception that one might expect on a first encounter.

It so happened that the temple was Yang Jing's ancestral shrine, where generations had offered incense. The family had always delighted in almsgiving and doing other good works. For the most part, the younger generation of sons and nephews made their living as Confucian scholars.

Additionally, my quest was facilitated by the approval of masters Yuefeng and Wuzong. All of the town's benevolent people of faith came to help; even Zi Yanzhi, the local aboriginal magistrate,[54] came to meet me. Everything worked out perfectly, with reciprocal affection and respect on all sides.

Receiving the tonsure at Fang'guang

This town, once wholly unknown to me, had now become deeply familiar. Once my monastic equipment had been supplied, I wanted to return to Jizu Mountain immediately for my ordination; however, the pious local almsgivers couldn't bear to part with me.

In 1632,[55] at the beginning of the ninth lunar month, a retired Dharma master named Liangru passed through Luomajing on his way back to the provincial capital. He had given a seminar on Buddhist scriptures in Yongchang county. At Luomajing, he was staying at the Eastern Mountain Great Realization Temple.

---

53. Western Mountain Radiance Temple

54. Aboriginal magistrates were placed in charge of China's border regions to oversee non-Han ethnic groups like the Miao (*Hmong*) and central Asian peoples.

55. year five of the Chongzhen reign

The Rambling Story of a Dream

I talked things over with Yuefeng: "These pious benefactors insist on keeping me here, but their hospitality prevents me from fulfilling my intention to be ordained. I'm thinking of going with Dharma Master Liangru to be tonsured; I can act as his attendant and request his teachings as we travel. But I'm worried that I'd be violating my vow to receive ordination on Mount Jizu—it would mean failure to keep my promise to retired abbot Dali. What should I do?"

Yuefeng's advice was, "Liangru belongs to the Jiguang lineage;[56] formerly, he served as a Jiguang abbot for three years.[57] The Buddhist name that you were given is also from the Jiguang lineage. If you are ordained by Master Liang, although you wouldn't be at the Jizu hermitage, you would still be the former abbot Dali's Dharma-grandson. Therefore, since they are of the same lineage, you'll be fulfilling your vow without failing to keep your promise. You should get moving right away—don't dither around indecisively."

His words convinced me. Yuefeng and I left the Fang'guang Temple, descended via the western ridge, and hiked up to the Eastern Mountain Great Realization Temple. There, I made obeisance to Master Liangru and only ventured the explanation that I had come to pay my respects to the venerable monk, as I didn't want to appear impudent and request the tonsure at our first meeting. After obtaining Master Liangru's gracious permission, we moved from the Western Mountain Radiance Temple.

The next day, I burned incense and entreated Liangru to give me the tonsure.[58]

---

56. Liangru was ordained by Sanmei Jiguang (1580–1645).

57. Three years is the normal term for an abbot to serve.

58. *Pravrajya* is the ceremony of going forth whereby an aspirant becomes a novice monk. Head-shaving is part of this ritual.

Receiving the tonsure

Smiling, he replied, "Last night, I dreamt that I saw a monk wearing a kāṣāya who was accompanied by a multitude of followers. He told me that his hair had grown out and begged me to shave his head. Today, I am complying with this predestined request.

"You were a monk in a previous existence and will carry on my work of propagating the Dharma and benefitting all sentient beings. You shall take the name Duti, with the courtesy name Shaoru.[59] Select a propitious date for the ceremony, prepare the five monastic robes, and you can receive the five fundamental precepts."

I felt deeply contrite that I had waited so long for my going forth. Fortunately, the stars showed that my intention was deeply rooted in previous lifetimes. I had my fortune cast and picked the fifth day of the tenth lunar month for the ceremony. When that day arrived, pious men and women passed through the town streets and hiked up the mountain one after the other to attend the joyous event.

I was feeling nervous because no one was there to support me at this crucial moment in my life. As I wandered aimlessly out of the temple gates, who did I run into but Chengzhuo! Two years had passed since our parting at Sanying. Seeing each other again was such a lucky coincidence that it seemed prearranged.

"Where have you come from?" I asked.

He replied, "From Baotai Mountain in Yongchang prefecture. I'd like to join Dharma Master Liangru's entourage as an attendant. Last night, I reached the base of the mountain and found out that he was staying here at the temple. The news was that today, he would be

---

59. The name signifies that Jianyue will be continuing Master Liangru's mission.

initiating a Daoist. Ha! They were talking about none other than Huanji!"

We beamed at one another, marveling at the unfathomable links of causality that had brought us together again. Between nine and eleven AM, the Dharma seat was set up and the ceremony of robing, head-shaving, and receiving the five precepts got underway.

A crowd of men and women encircled the Dharma seat, watching the proceedings as though the Buddhist initiate were their own next of kin. Sighing, they seemed unable to part with the one who was going forth. After the vegetarian meal offering was over, they finally dispersed and went their separate ways. As they journeyed home, all that could be heard was the sound of the Buddha's name repeated over and over again.

I am requested to turn the Dharma Wheel.[60]

On the evening of the next day, Yuefeng told me, "In this area, there are many pious Buddhists who keep the precepts and recite scriptures, but I've never heard of any monks who preach and give lectures. If you, the monk Shaoru, are willing to give lectures on Buddhist texts, you can request Master Liangru's gracious permission. By organizing a massive seminar to mark your tonsure ceremony, the destiny that brought you here will never be forgotten. Doesn't a starving person who is given a delicious meal hunker down and eat to satiety? Adding another course will round out the meal perfectly!"

I submitted Yuefeng's proposal to senior Dharma Master Liangru, also showing my willingness to act as the retreat

---

60. *i.e.*, teaching the Dharma. The Buddha is said to have turned the wheel of Dharma thrice.

leader. Liangru gave permission for me to lecture on the Lotus Sutra.⁶¹ Thus, a Buddhist seminar was set for the tenth of the month. We borrowed everything needed for the assembly grounds from the Aboriginal Magistrate Zi Yanzhi; the local folk voluntarily contributed food and money.

By day, I simultaneously acted as the retreat head and guest prefect; by night, I made a close study of the sūtra so that I could lecture on it the following day. I entrusted Master Chengzhuo with the duties of cashier and attendance registrar,⁶² while outside purchasing was Master Yuefeng's job. Every day, the fourfold assembly⁶³ in attendance was enormous. Everyone who came got three full meals consisting of rice congee⁶⁴ and vegetarian dishes. The assembly closed on the eighth day of the twelfth lunar month. The leftover monies and rice were given away to benefit the myriad sentient beings. This, too, increased the faith of our attendees.

A Dharma talk at Qiyun Temple

On the ninth day of the first month of the lunar year, I bid farewell to the crowd of almsgivers and Dharma protectors. On the tenth, I set out with Master Liangru. We reached Langqiong county on the fifteenth day of the month and stayed at the Miaozong Temple. Unfortunately, we couldn't rejoin Xiao Anchu because he lived too far away. As soon as Yang Shaoxian was informed of the situation, he came to

---

61. *Saddharmapuṇḍarīka-sūtra* [Skt.]

62. *siku, neiqin*

63. The fourfold assembly of Buddhist disciples: monks, nuns, laymen, and laywomen

64. Congee was not the thin gruel that is served in Chinese restaurants; it was a thick, toothsome porridge.

meet us and escorted us to his literati villa, where we could stay during the New Year holiday.

A Way-friend by the name of Bianzhou saw that as soon as I had been ordained, I had immediately initiated a massive preaching seminar wherein I acted as both lecturer and organizer. Bianzhou was from Heqing prefecture; he was a monk at the Qiyun hermitage on Longhua Mountain. Greatly impressed, he formed the pious intention of inviting Master Liangru to come to the Qiyun hermitage and give a talk on the *Śūraṅgama Sūtra*. Master Liangru generously agreed to donate his time and energy for the seminar.

After the Lantern Festival on the fifteenth day of the first month, I said goodbye to Yang Shaoxian and to the many old friends with whom we had spent the holiday. Seeing that they couldn't dissuade me from going, they pressed money upon me for travelling expenses. I adamantly refused their gifts, but seeing their disappointment, I finally agreed to take a little bit just to please them. When Master Liangru saw how indifferent I was to financial gain, he knew that I had eradicated the spiritual obstacle of avarice, and his affection for me grew stronger.

Responding to questions concerning the Dharma at Lijiang

On the twenty-second day of the month, we arrived at the Qiyun hermitage. Magistrate Mu, the aboriginal official of Lijiang prefecture, was a devout believer in the Three Jewels. Local regulations prohibited him from leaving his post, but as soon as he heard that a virtuous Way-friend and a Dharma master were coming to Heqing prefecture, he sent out a messenger to request that we pay him a visit at his home in Lijiang. Thus, an invitation was respectfully presented to Master Liangru, and I accompanied the venerable monk as his attendant.

Lijiang prefecture is bounded on the east by the Golden Sands River[65] and on the west by the Blackwater River;[66] it adjoins Jianchuan on its southern border and is located next to Tibet[67] in the north. The aboriginal magistrate's judiciary mansion had been built leaning against the feet of snowy mountains. Silver peaks towered up into the void, with verdant woodlands blanketing the earth below. We stayed there for half a month, responding to questions on the Buddha-Dharma as they arose.

Invoking the purity rules for the first time

On the eighteenth day of the second lunar month, we bade the magistrate farewell and went back to Heqing prefecture. There, the seminar on the Śūraṅgama Sūtra began on the twentieth day. I had the honor of being chosen as the rear hall head.[68] The monk Liaoran from Jianchuan, who resided at the Ten Thousand Buddhas Temple[69] on Shishi Mountain, was assigned to act as the head seat.[70] In his youth, Liaoran

---

65. Jinsha River
66. Heishui River
67. the territory of Tubo
68. *houtang*: A senior monk, who acts as an advisor to the head seat monk and oversees monastic discipline, is seated on the platform adjoining the rear door of a saṃgha hall. Crowds of monastics attended temple retreats. To accommodate them, they were divided into groups and seated on separate platforms. A supervisor was assigned to each group to maintain discipline.
69. Wanfo Temple
70. *shouzuo*: see appendices.

had visited every Buddhist lecture hall in Jiang'nan[71] to learn about the Dharma.

During the seminar, the four class heads took turns as lecturers. When it was Dharma Master Liaoran's turn to speak on the second fascicle,[72] his exegesis overstepped the sūtra's original meaning; he even had the impudence to repudiate and belittle Master Liangru, the presiding monk.[73] The assembly refused to condone such headstrong behavior. Yiyun, the west hall class leader,[74] spoke up indignantly.

His words spurred me to action. Impulsively, I took the floor of the lecture hall and revealed Liaoran's errors to the assembly. According to the rules of purity,[75] he should be severely punished. When Liangru, my tonsure master, got wind of the disruption, he came down to find out what had happened.

The assembled listeners told him, "The head seat has been trying to hoodwink us and lead us astray, while the rear hall is frank and upright and put him in his place. Neither of them went to you to report the incident. Master, we entreat you to show compassion and pardon them."

Addressing the head seat, Liangru said, "The meaning of the second fascicle is eminently clear and easily understood. By slandering both the scripture and the Dharma, you have provoked the ire of your listeners. You must examine your conscience regarding this incident."

---

71. The region south of the Yangtze River. It boasted many great temples and prominent monks.

72. wherein the Buddha explains to Ananda the difference between noumenon and phenomenon

73. *zhengzuo*

74. *xitang*: see appendices.

75. The Rules of Purity regulate monastic affairs that are not covered in the Vinaya. One such set of rules was formulated by the Tang-dynasty monk Baizhang.

To me, he said, "You've acted without my authority in denouncing someone and then meting out punishment for violating the purity rules. Strictly speaking, you should receive a heavy penalty, but those who witnessed the altercation are in favor of letting you off with a lighter one. You must burn a stick of incense and kneel until it is finished."[76]

He then addressed the assembly of monks: "Shaoru, the rear hall, was conscientiously upholding and protecting the sanctity of the sūtra and the Dharma. In the future, he will become a prominent saṃgha leader. He knows that monastic rules must be strictly followed but does not understand how to treat people mercifully by allowing them to keep face and retain their dignity."[77]

I first find out about the Vinaya.

One day, a few newly-ordained monastics came to our hermitage to attend Dharma lectures. We were disgusted by the group's vulgar, worldly manners.

Master Liangru admonished them: "The first step in going forth is receiving the ten *śrāmaṇera* precepts;[78] after that, novices can undertake full ordination in the rite of *upasampadā*.[79]

"Whether moving or stationary, sitting or lying down, proper monastics always exhibit dignity and composure.

---

76. Incense was used to time meditation sessions; here, it is burnt to time penitential kneeling.

77. Here, Hongyi has inserted a comment: "Liangru was only a run-of-the-mill monk, but in this case, his judgement shows tact and discretion."

78. to abstain from killing, stealing, sexual intercourse, lying, taking intoxicants, dancing or playing music, wearing ornaments or cosmetics, sleeping on an elevated bed, eating after midday, and touching money or precious objects (*Śrāmaṇera-saṃvara* [Skt])

79. Literally, "to approach the ascetic tradition." The full precepts are also referred to as the *bhikṣu* precepts.

The Rambling Story of a Dream

If you neither uphold the *bhikṣu* precepts nor preserve the prescribed demeanor, you cannot call yourselves monks; moreover, your flawed character defiles and dishonors the gateway to the Buddhist teachings."

While this was happening, I was standing next to Liangru as his attendant. Hearing the master's warning, I made obeisance to Liangru and said, "Master, please confer the bhikṣu precepts upon me so that I can become a fully-qualified monastic."

To my request, he replied, "I am a monk, a Dharma teacher.[80] In order to receive the full precepts, you must ask a Vinaya master to help you."

"Do you know any Vinaya masters?" I pursued.

The master returned, "The Vinaya lineage of Buddhism has nearly ceased to be transmitted. In Nanjing, Vinaya Master Guxin[81] was authorized to carry out ordination rites. Because his mission was to promote and rejuvenate a declining tradition, he was honored as the Vinaya Patriarch. He has already passed into *nirvāṇa*. Of his many ordained disciples, only the monk Sanmei[82] is still propagating the Vinaya tradition. Sanmei is currently in Jiang'nan."

Hearing this, I told him, "Then, I'll go to Jiang'nan to receive full ordination, and then come back here and continue serving as your attendant."

Liangru replied, "Ha! You speak of travelling to such a remote place as though it were a snap!"

But I continued doggedly, "Master, you just said that those who haven't received the full precepts[83] aren't real

---

80. *fashi*: Dharmabhāṇaka [Skt.]

81. Guxin is the courtesy name of Ruxin (1541–1615), who held ordinations in over thirty locations and had nearly ten thousand disciples.

82. The Chinese name is a transliteration of *samādhi* [Skt].

83. Monks receive 250 precepts, while 348 vows are conferred upon nuns.

monks. I relinquished Daoism and took refuge in the teachings of Sakyamunī in order to become a monk. What's the use of having a shaven head if I can't be a full-fledged monk?!"

Liangru remained silent and did not respond to my entreaty. I withdrew and left him.

After that, I brought the matter up regularly and was met each time with the same silence from Master Liangru. The Dharma retreat came to a close on the eighth day of the fourth lunar month. That afternoon, I once again went to the abbot's quarters to request a leave of absence.

Seeing that I was absolutely determined to go to the Jiang'nan region, he finally relented. "You are compelled by the force of your karma. Whether this journey brings you good fortune or hardship, you're still determined to go. All right, go!"

At the same time, several other people who wanted to make the trip with me also requested a leave of absence.

Master Liangru wryly observed: "You're just starting out on your journey, and already, so many people want to accompany you! If you learn the Dharma well, you will generate spiritual friendship;[84] if your learning is slipshod and misguided, you'll just become the boss of a pack of charlatans."

I saluted him with thanks: "I am indebted to you for your compassionate assurance that my spiritual efforts will someday bear the fruit of enlightenment.[85] I will heed your warning and strive to promote admirable fellowship."

---

84. *kalyāṇamitra* [Skt.]

85. *ryakarana*: The Buddha's assurance to his followers that their efforts will eventually result in supreme enlightenment

The Rambling Story of a Dream

Setting off on foot in search of a Vinaya master

In 1633, the sixth year of the Chongzhen imperial reign, I was thirty-two years old. On the eighth day of the fourth lunar month, I departed from the Qiyun hermitage between the third and fifth hours of the afternoon. That night, after a twenty-five *li*[86] trek, I came to a small hermitage, where I spent the night.

Midway through the second lunar month, Chengzhuo went to Mount Jizu. Our plan was to meet in Dali prefecture at the San'ta Temple[87] on the twentieth day of the fourth lunar month. I arrived according to plan, but there was no sign of Chengzhuo. The next day, I went to visit the Gantong Temple.

Chengzhuo finally arrived. Thereafter, we kept one another company for the entire journey south. After travelling for four days, we reached the Beiyan Guniao Temple, where I ran into an old friend from my former life as a lay person. He had become a monk and was a temple resident. When we met, he was busy handing out free cups of tea.[88]

Astonished to see me, he exclaimed, "So, you've become a monk and are out on a pilgrimage! If I weren't so old, I'd go with you!"

I advised him to stay at the temple and focus on purifying his karma, instead. By observing the precepts, showing filial devotion to his Buddhist master and parents, exercising compassion, and performing commendable actions, he would generate abundant merit. There was no need for the distraction of a long trip.

---

86. around eight miles
87. the Three Pagodas of the Chongsheng Temple
88. In some areas of southern China, during the sultry summer months, free cups of tea were offered to townspeople and temple worshippers as an act of compassion.

Moved by my words, he vowed to devote the rest of his life to chanting the Buddha's name. I stayed at the temple for ten days, then took my leave and continued on my journey.

A farewell salute to ancestral tombs

By the second day of the fifth lunar month, I could see Baiyun county in the distance—my hometown lay before my eyes. Ten miles from the city, I found lodgings at Jinshan Temple.

I reflected on my past lapses: I hadn't taken care of my parents, nor had I been present at my uncle's funeral. That entire night, my tears never dried. My thoughts also turned to the two younger brothers whom I had abandoned seven years ago. What miserable fate had befallen them? Who would support them now? There was no telling what would happen to me once I left the area and continued on my long journey, so it was imperative that I see my family now.

At daybreak, I told Chengzhuo what was weighing on my heart, and then set off to visit my relatives. No sooner had I stepped outside and walked a few paces than I stopped dead in my tracks and heaved a sigh. Thoughts of what loomed ahead and what had happened in the past revolved in my mind.

Then, it occurred to me that if I succumbed to family concerns at this crucial point in my life, I would fall into the powerful snare of their karma. Not only would I be prevented from fulfilling my goals of receiving full ordination and practising spiritual cultivation, but I would also have no means of repaying a debt of gratitude to the parents who had given birth to me and my uncle who had graciously taken me under his wing.

Every individual life, I reflected, is shaped by a unique set of circumstances. What happens to humans in their present earthly life is determined by what they have done in previous lifetimes. Wealth or poverty, happiness or misery, longevity or untimely death—all are manifestations of their past actions. Hence, in spite of the deep bond between father and son, one of them cannot take on the other's karmic burden.

My greatest regret was never having returned to see my uncle: I had disregarded his benevolence and righteousness and shown him no compassion. But there was nothing to be done about it now. The only way to help my family members was to direct the merit accrued by my spiritual cultivation back to them.

I wiped my tears dry as I walked around the city's outer perimeter, looking towards the western hills of Yun'nan, where lay my family's ancestral tombs. I knelt and touched the ground with my forehead. My heart was wrung with sorrow, my legs were so weak that I could hardly get up. Finally, I forced myself to hurry away. Arriving in Guangtong county, I spent the night at an ancient temple.

Setting deep emotions aside and cutting off family ties

The next day, on the road to Lufeng county, I ran into a relative named Zhou Zhibin, who was returning to Chuxiong after a trip to the provincial capital.

He caught sight of me from afar and called out in a loud voice, "Xu Chongxiao, where are you living now? When did you become a monk? Where are you going?"

I called back, "I was ordained on Mount Jizu. Right now, I'm on my way to Jiang'nan[89] to receive my final vows and to practise and study Buddhism."

---

89. Jiang'nan refers to the prosperous area located south of the lower reaches of the Yangtze River.

"Do you have any letters that you'd like me to carry back home and deliver for you?"[90] he inquired.

All that I could say was: "I can't possibly express my thoughts and feelings about my family in writing. But I'm concerned about my two younger brothers. Can you please look after them for me?"

While I was answering my relative's questions, my feet never stopped pacing along the road. He asked me something else; choked with sobs, I was so stricken with sorrow that I couldn't respond. My kinsman stood watching me until I was far off in the distance. At last, he turned and continued on his way.

Observing this scene, Chengzhuo protested, "Since you aren't going back to see your family, couldn't you at least have given him a verbal message to convey?"

My reply was, "Cutting off family ties with a blunt knife draws less blood; talking would only provoke a storm of emotions. The ancients say: 'The heart is as unyielding as iron; aspirations are firm and upright. Love is unforgettable; it is hard to master the subtlest, most esoteric principles.'"

Crossing through the Biji and Jinma mountain passes

We continued onward for several days. With the provincial capital in sight, we entered the Biji Pass.[91] The peaks and ridges of this mountain pass dominate the surrounding hills; they are of surpassing elegance. They overlook Lake Dianchi, an expanse of blue that covers innumerable

---

90. It was a common practice to entrust letters to people who happened to be passing through an addressee's location.

91. Blue Chicken Pass

The Rambling Story of a Dream

hectares. We took a boat across Lake Dianchi. On the opposite shore, we landed in the provincial capital.

That night, we stayed outside the city walls at the Maitreya Temple. The friends who were accompanying us made plans to stay there for a few days and visit all of the local temples, but I was worried about running into old friends and family members, which would hinder our progress.

Early the next day, we went to Songhua Dam, emerged from the Jinma Pass,[92] and finally reached the Banqiao post-house,[93] where we spent the night. Chengzhuo's lay family lived in Xundian prefecture. He had embarked on the monastic life[94] in Yanglin at the Nazhai Guanyin hermitage. There was a shortcut to this temple, making it only a short distance from our present location. Chengzhuo invited the entire group to go with him and pay their respects to his master before continuing on our long journey.

We crossed the Tu'er Pass and spent the night at the Heyou hermitage. The next morning, we arrived at our destination. Chengzhuo's teacher was both virtuous and kind; the master's elder brother was simple and unaffected. Both practised spiritual cultivation. As soon as they saw us, they welcomed us joyfully. The brothers treated us with great hospitality and insisted that we prolong our visit. We stayed there for half a month, and finally bid the two kindly monks goodbye.

---

92. Golden Horse Pass

93. In ancient China, imperial couriers would change horses and find accommodations at relay stations that were set up at regular intervals throughout the country.

94. *chujia* [Ch]

An arhat lantern

We purchase an arhat lantern.

After several days on the road, we arrived at Qujing prefecture and came to Poqin Mountain, the site where Meng Huo, a southern rebel chieftain, finally offered his allegiance to the great Shu statesman and tactician Zhuge Liang.[95] We spent the night at an ancient temple in the area.

I told our group of travelling companions, "On this long journey, we aren't going to act like the usual itinerant monks who wander about sightseeing and admiring the scenery while neglecting their spiritual practice. We'll purchase an arhat lamp:[96] the top part serves as a lamp, while oil is stored at the bottom. During the daytime, the lamp can be carried on a shoulder-pole; at night, it will serve as illumination.

"Every evening, we will take turns keeping watch. Between 7 and 9 PM after the evening meal, we will light the lamp. Then, we will all sit around it and read whichever scripture we are currently studying or reflect upon its contents. At midnight, we will end the session. We will observe this rule throughout our trip."

Everyone approved of my suggestion and complied with the new schedule.

---

95. Zhuge Liang (181–234 CE), the renowned chancellor and regent of the Shu-Han state, is a protagonist in the *Romance of the Three Kingdoms*, a fourteenth-century historical novel. Meng Huo, a semi-historical tribal leader, is also depicted in the *Romance of the Three Kingdoms*.

96. In Buddhist tradition, the Eighteen Arhats were disciples of the Buddha who became adepts. Most Chinese temples have statues of the arhats, one of whom carries a lamp.

The Rambling Story of a Dream

We travel through Guansuoling and cross the Pan River.

We came to Pingyiwei and emerged from the Dian'nan[97] scenic area that shares a border with Guizhou province. We went through Yizikong[98] and entered Pu'anwei City. We continued for several days and passed through Guansuoling, an extremely lofty and steep ridge of mountains[99] with a periphery spanning over a hundred *li*.[100] A military base is located on the ridgetop, as well as the Guansuo Temple.

After several more days of travel, we crossed the Pan River.[101] The mountain road is winding and crooked; both ascent and descent are perilous. All at once, a torrential downpour inundated the trail. In the mountain valleys, small rivulets turned into waterfalls and emitted a thunderous roar. Deep ditches flooded, causing rivers of water to emerge along the winding mountain road, while a fierce gale blew at us with cyclone force from all directions.

We could barely remain standing. Water poured down our necks and saturated our lower garments. We inched forward, stepping from side to side horizontally as though straddling flotation bags. When we loosened our belts to release some of the water that had accumulated in our robes,

---

97. Dian'nan is an ancient name for Yun'nan.

98. Yizi lies in Panzhou province. It is called Yizikong because Confucius passed through the area while travelling south. *Kong* is the ancient philosopher's family name.

99. The highest peak of Guansuoling lies 2,138 meters above sea level. Ancient postal routes passed through the area, which is also part of the imperial defense system.

100. over 31 miles

101. The Beipan River flows through Guizhou and Yun'nan provinces; it is part of the great Pearl River basin.

Guansuoling

streams poured swiftly downwards as though a dike had been breached. This went on for quite a while. The icy cold penetrated our bones and sinews.

To boost my comrades' morale, I told them that the ancients were so intent on getting to a place where they could study the Dharma that the possibility of dying along the way never fazed them at all.

"Later on, when we recount this adventure," I continued, "just think how heroic we'll appear!"

In the thick of the storm, everyone broke into a smile. By evening, leaning on our canes and helping one another move forward through the fierce downpour, we finally reached the foot of the mountain.

We spent the night at the Dayuan Temple. There, we met a monk from Jiang'nan. We inquired about travel conditions on the road ahead.

He answered: "This is the worst time for journeying on foot. There are gangs of ruffians everywhere who prey upon honest travelers. They won't bother anyone wearing patched monastic robes and carrying meditation cushions made of rushes, but if you don't look like poor monks, I fear that you will never reach your destination.

"Friends, my advice is that you trade in your luggage for humbler equipment. That will ensure you a peaceful journey."

We rested at the temple for ten days, and then crossed the Beipan River by means of an iron-cable bridge. We beheld steep cliffs, a profusion of forests and bamboo thickets, and the surging river rushing like an arrow below. This bridge is an important crossing in the Yun'nan-Guizhou Plateau.

On the road to Anzhuangwei

The next day, we reached the mountain path leading to the Anzhuangwei garrison. Tortuous and zigzagging, the precipitous road was bumpy with piles of sand. Our shoes kept slipping off our feet—unbeknownst to us, the soles were worn straight through. There was nothing to be done about it, so we tossed them aside and continued barefoot. We walked on for dozens of miles, only stopping at nightfall. Our feet were so swollen that our heels were no longer visible; we experienced such intense pain that our feet seemed scorched by fire and pierced by sharp awls.

In the middle of the night, it suddenly occurred to us that we were penniless in an area where there was only a solitary hermitage and a path winding through open, untenanted country. Since there was nowhere to beg for alms, we had to get moving promptly at dawn the following morning.

We reflected that in the pursuit of fame and riches, lay people willingly endured long stretches of toil and hardship. Our own goal was to become ordained and seek the path leading to liberation from suffering. Were we going to abandon our initial determination to seek enlightenment just because we lacked footgear?

The next day, we again forced ourselves to keep on going. At first, our progress was laborious, and we winced whenever our heels touched the ground. After a while, leaning on our canes and limping along, we managed to travel five or six miles. Numbness set in: our feet didn't seem to belong to us and we no longer felt any pain. The road afforded no rest stops; by evening, we had trodden over fifty *li*.[102]

---

102. over 15 miles

I copy a sūtra commentary

We spent the night at the Anzhuangwei hermitage. The next day, we obtained grass shoes from almsgivers. When we tried them on, they cut into the chafed, blistered skin on our feet, but we took no notice of the pain.

A ruffianly fellow had attached himself to our party. He continued following us for several days. Even when we took a break or stayed overnight somewhere, he never left us for a moment. One afternoon, we came to a small river spanned by a single-plank bridge that extended about eight yards. Chengzhuo and the other members of our group went first, and I walked slowly behind them.

The shady character tailed me. Right in the middle of the bridge, I suddenly shouted. Startled, the ruffian fell off the bridge and plopped into the water.

I pointed at him, saying, "From now on, you need to turn over a new leaf and start being an honest person."

He blushed and climbed up the bank. Averting his face, he slunk off on a different path.

I copy a sūtra commentary at the Zhishui hermitage.

No one in our group ever considered the many kinds of hardship that we endured to be suffering.

Summer passed and now it was fall. At the beginning of the tenth lunar month, we finally reached Huguang Wugangzhou and found lodgings at the Zhishui hermitage. The monastery head Yihui[103] was deeply focused upon the Way.[104] As soon as he found out that we had come all the way from Yun'nan, he invited us to spend the entire winter at the temple.

---

103. 'Strange Grass'
104. the Buddhist path to liberation

The Rambling Story of a Dream

One day, he invited me to his chamber for tea. On the table, there was a copy of the *Fahua zhiyin*.[105] That title had become fixed in my memory when I was in Yun'nan, because I had heard my teacher praise it highly. I immediately wanted to borrow the book and copy it, but unfortunately had neither brush nor paper. Yihui's younger tonsure brother, whose Dharma name was Zhongli, loved to study and understood my heart's desire. He provided me with all of the supplies I needed for my task.

Every day that winter, it snowed incessantly. The room in which I was staying was spacious and wide open to the elements: the North wind blew gustily through the windows, and I was only clad in a patched monk's robe. I copied the manuscript sitting hunched over on one of the plank beds that were assigned to itinerant monks. Although my fingers were stiff with cold, the skin chapped and broken, and my brush kept icing over, I never rested for a moment. Marveling at my steadfast determination and diligence to learn, the two tonsure brothers felt increasing affection and respect for me and gave me a padded jacket. I accepted their gift with a certain chagrin: I had never worn a cotton-padded coat in my entire life.

A few of our travelling companions bade us farewell and went on to Chaohai, while Chengzhuo and Juexin stayed behind as my companions.

The vassal state of Wugangzhou is the Prince of Min's domain. Yan Li, a member of the prince's royal clan, was an afficionado of calligraphy and painting and frequently met with Master Yihui. In the middle of the tenth lunar month, he tramped through the snow to visit the hermitage, car-

---

105. "A Companion to the Lotus Sutra," *Saddharma Puṇḍarīka Sūtra* [Skt]

rying paper for ink painting. He attached a blank sheet of paper to a wall inside the monastery, intending to paint an illustration of the poem: "Snowfall on a frigid river: in a solitary boat, an old man clad in grass coat and conical hat fishes alone."[106] Yan Li tried several times to do a preliminary charcoal sketch, but remained indecisive.

I stood next to him watching. Commenting, I told him, "Before setting brush to paper, an artist must formulate a clear mental image of the painting. Once the brush is in motion, there is no time left for pondering or hesitation. Only then can the brush convey a subject's special charm. I fear that by irresolutely overthinking and grappling for a plan, you'll lose the scene's natural sparkle."

He turned and looked at me: "Easier said than done. Can you paint this?"

I smiled and told him, "Well, I only know a little bit about painting."

At that, he handed me the brush, saying, "Give it a try!"

Receiving the brush, I first mentally envisioned the overall design, and then I flourished the brush, completed the painting, and finally rested the brush on the table.

Lord Yan was deeply impressed and told Yi Hui, "This hermitage has quite a few adepts hidden among the monks. Keep this painting and hang it up!"

After that, he often came to visit and would sit conversing with me. He wrote three calligraphy scrolls with his own hand and presented one to me and the other two to Chengzhuo and Juexin. Lord Yan told us all about the far-flung travels that he had undertaken to visit distinguished people.

---

106. a renowned Tang-dynasty poem by Liu Zongyuan (773–819 CE)

The Rambling Story of a Dream

Attending a seminar on the Śūraṅgama Sūtra at the Liangjia hermitage

On the fifth day of the first month of the new year, Dharma Master Heyi held a seminar on the *Śūraṅgama Sūtra* at the Liangjia hermitage, which was located sixty *li*[107] from the Zhishui hermitage. Master Zhongli came and invited us to attend. Chengzhuo had never read the Śūraṅgama Sūtra, so he went to the Wutai hermitage at Baoqing prefecture to pay his respects to Grandmaster Zhuanyu.[108] He intended to wait until the seminar was over before coming to the Liangjia hermitage to meet us.

I arrived at the hermitage with Master Zhongli and Juexin. There were only twenty-some attendees, each of whom paid a bushel of rice and a tael of silver to join the assembly. Master Zhongli duly handed over his payment; as for myself and Juexin, we had neither rice nor money. We'd only come along to enjoy a temple visit, bringing nothing more than the monastic robes that we wore and our reed cushions.

Master Zhongli put in a word on our behalf with the temple monks. Once they learned that we were from impoverished Yun'nan, they agreed to exempt us from paying the money and rice and graciously allowed us to attend the seminar free of charge.

I told Juexin, "These monks are teaching the Buddha-Dharma as an alms-offering; however, food and drink are provided by utilizing each participant's seminar registration fee. We can't just take advantage of their generosity without making some contribution."

---

107. about 19 miles

108. Zhuanyu Guanheng, the eminent Chan master "Honest Fool" (1579–1646).

I need formal equipment to enter the lecture hall

Thus, both of us volunteered to do odd jobs during the assembly. We collected and washed bowls and chopsticks after meals, swept the floor, and carried buckets of water on shoulder poles. There was no need for anyone to assign chores—we willingly got things done whenever we had free time. On the first day of the fourth lunar month, the seminar came to an end. Zhongli decided to remain at the temple. Juexin and I took our leave and went to Baoqing prefecture,[109] where we stayed at the Da Bao'en Temple as itinerant monks.

I need formal equipment to enter the lecture hall.[110]

We found out that Dharma Master Ziru, one of the temple monks, was from Yun'nan, so we visited him and paid our respects. We told him about our ordination plans and recounted the adventures we'd had on our southward journey. Upon hearing our story, Master Ziru started calling me "younger tonsure brother." I wondered at the new mode of address.

He explained, "I'm from Jianchuan and was ordained as a monk at Shishi Mountain.[111] As a junior monk, I studied Buddhist texts and doctrine under venerable Dharma Master Liangru. I took refuge under the old master for six years, during which time I assimilated his profound Buddhist wisdom. Since then, I haven't been in touch with him at all.

"When I saw you today, Master Shaoru, I felt as though I were seeing my old tonsure master again. According to our shared Buddhist lineage, it is right for me to address

---

109. now Shaoyang city in Hunan

110. *kāṣāya*: a monastic's patched robe. Here, a lecturer's elaborate robe is implied.

111. Stone Chamber Mountain: 'mountain' signifies 'monastery.'

The Rambling Story of a Dream

you as younger tonsure brother. In Yun'nan, which sūtras did Master Liangru expound?"

I replied, "Under the tutelage of Master Liangru, we heard about the Lotus Sūtra and the Śūraṅgama Sūtra[112] but never grasped their profound meaning. He planted the seeds of future understanding."

Master Ziru then inquired, "From whence have you come today?"

"We've just come from the Liangjia hermitage at Wugangzhou. There, we attended Dharma Master Heyi's seminar on the Śūraṅgama Sūtra. Afterwards, we came here."

Master Ziru remarked, "Dharma Master Heyi is a Way-friend; we were classmates. You've come at the perfect time: Grandmaster Zhuanyu[113] has just written a treatise entitled "An Explanation of the Four Kinds of Reliance as Set Forth in the Śūraṅgama Sūtra."[114] Every Dharma protector and lay Buddhist who knows of this work is requesting that it be published and put into circulation.

"The Master has ordered me to hold a public exposition here at the temple. So far, over a hundred people have signed up to attend. Right now, we need someone to act as the rear hall trainer.[115] Younger brother, you can do this."

---

112. This sūtra, also known as the *Śūraṅgama* mantra, describes a form of meditation. Étienne Lamotte (1903–1983), a distinguished Belgian priest and professor, translated the text as *La concentration de la marche héroïque*.

113. The *Lingfeng zong lun* [Treatise on the Spirit Mountain Tradition], in which Master Ou'yi Zhixu (1599–1655) records his lifetime attainment as a spiritual practitioner, includes a eulogy on Master Zhuanyu, as well as the inscription on his stūpa.

114. The four bases of the Dharma referred to in the text may have been: to rely upon the Dharma rather than the teacher, to rely upon essential meaning rather than words, to rely upon wisdom rather than ordinary consciousness, and to rely upon accurate cognition rather than mere representation.

115. The training supervisor seated on the rear platform of the saṃgha hall. This duty was usually assigned to senior monks, who acted as advisors to the head seat.

I need formal equipment to enter the lecture hall

"Just assign me a place for my meditation mat and a hook to hang my robe on—that's good enough for me,"[116] I replied. "I wouldn't dare to fill a leadership position."

Master Ziru told me, "A lion cub has no need of excessive humility. I'll buy you the robe, shoes, and socks suitable for entering the lecture hall in an official capacity."

I replied, "I'll do it under two conditions: First, that I be allowed to wear my own patched robes and bring my own reed cushion into the saṃgha hall for sitting and reclining; Secondly, I implore the abbot not to send people over to ply me constantly with extra food. All I want is to listen to the sūtra teachings and partake of the "flavor" of the Dharma. I'm full of admiration for the Grandmaster—there's no need to offer me any additional favors."

But Ziru would not hear of such offhand treatment and insisted upon my wearing new clothing.

At that time, there was a resident monk named Yexi[117] who had signed up for the retreat. He had taken refuge under Grandmaster Zhuanyu[118] and had been with him for many years. The day after this exchange with Master Ziru, he went to the Wutai hermitage to pay the grandmaster a courtesy call. When the master asked him how the retreat arrangements were coming along, Yexi told him about my background and my earnest request to retain my humble status and equipment.

Upon hearing this, the Grandmaster responded, "As a

---

116. In a traditional monastic environment, a newly-admitted monk hangs his robes and clothing on a hook above his mat, which from then on is where he sleeps and lives. Thus, being assigned a hook for hanging up one's clothes signifies formal registration to attend a retreat.

117. 'Wild Brook'

118. In the *Lingfeng zong lun*, Master Zhuanyu is warmly praised.

The Rambling Story of a Dream

youth, I resided at the Wutai Zhulin Temple,[119] where I was a follower of Grandmaster Yuechuan.[120] I always attended Buddhist seminars wearing my kāṣāya and straw sandals[121] and bringing along my staff, bamboo hat, and cushion. Later on, I became an itinerant monk and visited Tiantai,[122] Nanyue,[123] as well as here in Baoqing[124] without ever changing my apparel or equipment. When a group of generous lay donors[125] built this temple, they knelt down on the ground with both hands held aloft in supplication to offer me new clothing and shoes. They entreated me to accept their gifts, insisting that they would continue kneeling until I changed into new clothes. Finally, I acceded to their wishes, since my doing so would quicken their religious faith.

"I always see Chan meditation monks who are unwilling to correct their own habitual tendencies that generate

---

119. Wutai Bamboo Forest Temple

120. 'Moon River'

121. Holmes Welch observes that by the twentieth century, so-called "straw" sandals were actually made of cloth. In her monograph on shoes in Buddhist monasteries, Ann Heirman notes that Daoxuan, the arbiter of Chinese Buddhist protocol, permitted various kinds of footwear, although straw sandals were worn without socks on journeys. Holmes Welch, *The Practice of Chinese Buddhism, 1900–1950* (Cambridge: Harvard University Press, 1973), 474, note 12. https://terebess.hu/zen/mesterek/Holmes-Welch-The-Practice.pdf

Ann Heirman, "Shoes in Buddhist Monasteries from India to China: From Practical Attire to Symbol," *Acta Orientalia Academiae Scientiarum Hungaricae* 69, no. 4 (2016): 436. http://www.jstor.org/stable/26424896.

122. Tiantai county is noted for Tiantai Mountain, a Buddhist holy site. Tiantai is located in modern Zhejiang province.

123. Nanyue (Mount Heng) is located in Hunan province. At the foot of the mountain stands the largest temple in southern China, the Grand Temple of Mount Heng (*Nanyue damiao*). It is the largest group of ancient buildings in Hunan Province.

124. Baoqing Temple, located in Ningbo city, Zhejiang province

125. *dānapati* [Skt]

I need formal equipment to enter the lecture hall

affliction[126] and hindrance. There's not a single one of them who doesn't crave good food and fine apparel. Someone who sticks to his principles and opts for simple austerity is a rarity.

"Hearing you talk about this monk from Yun'nan who refuses to be distracted from his spiritual path by external circumstances, I am reminded of myself in those days. Go back and tell Master Ziru to comply with his requests and not force him to abandon his resolve just to please a stodgy audience! That monk's example will serve as a lesson to those retreatants, reminding them to refrain from excessive attachments."

In accordance with the grandmaster's order, Master Ziru allowed me to keep my old robes and equipment. Among the retreat participants, some approved of my "unsophisticated simplicity," while others jeered at my "unorthodox, designedly attention-grabbing" appearance. I turned a deaf ear on both parties.

After the first three days of the seminar, the abbot ordered the four class leaders to give a series of sermons: in alternating sequence, each official would present six lectures. As it happened, the west hall head[127] left the temple to go on an errand, while the head seat[128] requested leave of absence due to illness. Of the four assembly leaders, only Master Kedu, the hall chief,[129] and I remained.

Kedu had received Dharma transmission from Grandmaster Wuxue[130] of Nanyue Jingzi peak in Hunan. Master Kedu was a monk of mellow, robust character who had a

---

126. *kleśa* [Skt]

127. A retired head priest staying at another monastery was placed in charge of the monks seated on the west temple platform.

128. *shouzuo*: rector

129. *tangzhu*: assistant instructor

130. 'No Study'

penchant for study. In terms of personal aspirations and mindset, we were kindred spirits: we treated one another with great mutual respect. Between the two of us, we had to cover "An Explanation of the Four Kinds of Reliance as Set Forth in the Śūraṅgama Sūtra" from the fourth chapter to the end. We took turns expounding the entire assigned text.

Paying a visit to Grandmaster Zhuanyu

When the assembly was over, Dharma Master Ziru led the participants to Wutai hermitage so that they could pay their respects to Grandmaster Zhuanyu and thank him for his treatise on the Śūraṅgama Sūtra.

When we arrived, the grandmaster was sitting cross-legged in meditation under a parasol. His nickname, in fact, was Sanju Daoren, the "Way-practitioner living under a parasol." After formally thanking the grandmaster, Master Ziru returned to the Bao'en Temple.

The grandmaster kept me with him under the parasol and offered me a meal: the vegetable dish consisted of a plate of bitter melon. Master Zhuanru took some with his chopsticks and told me to help myself. I picked up a piece of bitter melon with my chopsticks and put it in my mouth. It was so bitter that I gagged, yet I didn't dare to spit it out.

Noting my predicament, the grandmaster smiled and told me: "It tastes bitter at first, but later on, you'll find it sweet. Both religious practice and the process of finding spiritual friendship are like that, too."

I thanked him for imparting this wisdom.

The grandmaster then observed, "You have some strength of character. Where are you planning on going next?"

I replied, "I set off from Yun'nan with the intention of

meeting the Monk Sanmei and requesting ordination from him. After receiving the full precepts, I intend to travel and study as an itinerant monk."

"The Monk Sanmei is a genuine Vinaya master," the grandmaster allowed, "You can certainly receive the precepts from him.

He continued, "As for wandering around in search of wisdom, allow me to warn you that in the Buddhist monasteries of Jiang'nan,[131] regulations are lax and those who expound the scriptures tend to be haughty and overbearing. If you find such goings-on unsuitable, you'd best come back here. Don't abandon yourself to inappropriate practices and behavior. In the future, you are sure to become a pillar of the Dharma-gate."[132]

Master Zhuanyu immediately ordered an attendant to bring a set of literary works that he had composed and present them to me as a gift.

Once again, he cautioned me, urging: "You should master the proper conduct and spiritual practice that I teach."

Bowing reverently, I accepted the grandmaster's gift and counsel.

Pheasant Lake

The next day, it was arranged that Chengzhuo and I would go and visit the Grand Temple of Mount Heng.[133] We set off from Baoqing prefecture and traveled for five days. After passing through Yangliutang,[134] we climbed the back

---

131. regions south of the Yangtze River
132. Buddhist doctrine
133. the Nanyue Grand Temple
134. Willow Pond

mountain and toured Jiulongping[135] and Gudaping.

Alongside these plains lay a body of water called Pheasant Lake, so named when the Monk Sanmei visited it during his travels. As he stood on the lake's shore, a dragon that had been transformed into the shape of a pheasant emerged from the water fluttering its wings. Right away, Sanmei conferred the five precepts and the three refuges[136] upon the creature.

We also paid our respects to Buddhist temples in Maoping and other towns. We made a circuit around the mountains Tianzhu and Yanxia. Descending from Zhurong Peak, we arrived in front of the Grand Shrine of Mount Heng. There, we stayed in a hut where free tea was offered to wayfarers and local folk alike.

Taking an alternate route to Jiangxi

At the tea hut, we met an itinerant monk[137] and inquired about local travel conditions.

He cautioned us: "Right now, bandits are running rampant in places like Changde, Tanzhou, Gong'an, and Jingzhou, so all of these towns are closely guarded by the military. Unfortunately, the local magistrates and soldiery are corrupt and unscrupulous. They confiscate the luggage of travelling monks and arrest them on trumped-up charges, accusing them of spying. Such monks suffer injustice yet are unable to air their grievances; they must bear vexation and distress silently, with no hope of redress. Take heed, don't travel down the mountain!"[138]

---

135. Nine-Dragon Plain
136. The three Buddhist refuges are the Buddha, the Dharma and the Sangha.
137. a 'cloud-water' monk
138. Late Ming-dynasty political chaos forms a backdrop for much of the en-

An alternate route to Jiangxi

Upon hearing the monk's advice, Chengzhuo and I weren't the least bit daunted. If we stopped now, it would mean that we'd already travelled several thousand miles in vain—so much energy squandered for nothing! Thus, we asked the head of the temple to suggest an alternate route to our destination.

His advice was, "Everything now is in such a state of turmoil that it's best to make a temporary halt here and continue your journey once peace has been restored. Don't be so impatient to move on!"

I persisted: "I'm determined to keep going. Time waits for no one! I'd be deeply grateful if you could suggest an alternate route for us to take."

Finally, he relented and said, "There is another road, but it's extremely wild and unfrequented. Very few people pass that way due to its harsh mountainous terrain and deep ravines. The only way to get through the region is via Qianyang. Go towards Liling county, pass Pu'an Cihua Temple, and then ask the locals how to get to Wanzai county. Once you've reached Ruizhou prefecture, you'll be able to get to the provincial capital, Jiangxi. By taking that route, you can avoid chaotic areas that are aswarm with roving bandits."

Early the next morning, we set off along the route that the hermitage head had recommended. Just as he said, the entire way was mountainous and desolate, devoid of villages and human habitation. Sometimes, we'd take a morning meal and then travel until evening; at other times, we'd set off on an empty stomach. We never covered fewer than

---

suing narrative. Rebel bandits and corrupt officials threatened the populace, and since powerless intellectuals like monks often joined and even led local uprisings, they, too, were regarded with suspicion. See Harriet T. Zurndorfer. 1983. "Violence and Political Protest in Ming and Qing China." *International Review of Social History* 28 (3): 307. https://www.jstor.org/stable/44583728.

The Rambling Story of a Dream

seventy or eighty *li* every day.[139]

Visiting Lushan and paying our respects at the Donglin monastic community

After half a month's trek, our circuitous course brought us to the province of Jiangxi. We stayed at the Taxia Temple and rested for three days. After that, we went to De'an county and delighted in the grandeur of Mount Lu. We visited Guizong Temple,[140] as well as Kaixian, Wuru, and other temples.

One day, we came to Wansong hermitage.[141] Since evening was drawing nigh, we knocked on the door to register as itinerant monastics, but an irate temple monk slammed the gate shut and refused to let us in.

By then, the sky was growing dark and stars glittered aloft. We had to find somewhere else to shelter for the night and noticed a large rock overhang spanning an area of several yards that covered one side of the road. The three of us squeezed under it, spread out our cushions, and awaited the dawn.

After a while, the temple gates opened again and the same monk came out to drive us away. We heaved a mutual sigh, relegating the monk's gratuitous negativity to lack of karmic affinity. Rather than revile him, we just ignored him for the entire night, pitying his stupidity and adamantly refusing to budge.

The three of us arose before daybreak and continued

---

139. about twenty-five miles
140. originally the rustic home of the renowned calligrapher Wang Xizhi (303–361 AD)
141. Ten Thousand Pine hermitage

Visiting Lushan

on our way. We breakfasted at Douyeping, and then visited Shaigushi and Yangtianping, even getting to Jinzhuping. Close to sunset, we arrived at the Donglin Temple[142] and registered as itinerant monks.

The Chan meditation hall was located at the back. The hall designated for visiting monastics only consisted of three decrepit rooms. The area was insufferably overgrown, with foot-high weeds growing everywhere. The walls were caved in; the roof-tiles had fallen off; doors and windows no longer served as barriers to the elements.

The temple featured a beamless hall. We entered to worship the Buddha, only to find the renowned shrine littered with thick accumulations of dust and the filthy droppings of pigeons and sparrows. Chengzhuo and I swept the Buddha hall clean and placed our cushions to the left of the Buddha image. We discussed spending the entire night chanting the name of Amitābha Buddha, so as not to squander our precious time at the ancient White Lotus society temple.[143]

Much to our astonishment, the business office manager[144] emerged and reprimanded us for barging into the Buddha hall and spreading out our mats unbidden, without first announcing our intentions to the temple officials. Loudly berating us, he drove us out of the room and out to the main gate of the monastery.

An elderly monk who lived near the gate[145] offered us a

---

142. The Eastern Forest Temple is located in northern Jiangxi province. It was built in 386 CE by Huiyuan, the founder of the Pure Land sect.

143. The first White Lotus Society, located in the Donglin Temple of Mount Lu, was founded by the monk Huiyuan (334–416 CE).

144. *dangjia seng*: the head manager whose private office is located in the business department. *see* appendices.

145. This monk might have been a retired teacher or may have dealt with alms donations.

The Rambling Story of a Dream

meal and invited us to stay with him. Right away, the irate manager reemerged and upbraided the old monk. He then proceeded to splash water all over the ground, drenching the area so thoroughly that we could neither sit nor lie down. The three of us thanked the old monk and took our leave; we then exited through the temple gate.

I observed to Chengzhuo and Juexin: "Many lifetimes ago, we undoubtedly engendered negativity with that monastery official: his treatment of us today is the outcome of our previous offenses. Let us now think of him as a worthy spiritual guide who can help us to master the bodhisattva practice of refraining from hostility. Do not let this incident give rise to anger and resentment."

But this moral lesson did not solve the immediate problem facing us. Despite treating the setback with calm acceptance and forbearance, we still found ourselves outside with nowhere to spend the night.

Chengzhuo said, "On the way to this temple, I noticed a dense grove of trees by the road. We can pass the night there."

Retracing our steps, the thicket of trees turned out to be an ancient tomb. We spread out our mats and sat down. In that vast, utterly still, moonless wilderness, the dark was so intense that we couldn't even see our fingers when we held our hands right in front of our faces.

In the early hours of the night,[146] we were startled by a voice shouting, "Catch them!"

All around us, voices started crying: "Catch the thieves!!"

I told Chengzhuo and Juexin, "If they chase us down and grab us, laying murderous hands upon us, they won't bother to verify our guilt or innocence. The circumstances

---

146. between 6 and 10 PM

will look too incriminating to allow any protestations of innocence. Our fates will be sealed."

We awaited the dawn apprehensively. Finally, the horse bells of dispatch riders could be heard from afar. A major highway evidently lay somewhere in the vicinity. Knowing that, we felt somewhat reassured. The three of us emerged from the wood and came across someone laboring in a field. We asked him the reason for the previous night's massive outcry.

"Right now," he replied, "the grain in the fields is ripe. Everyone goes out and makes a huge commotion in order to scare thieves away."[147]

At that, all three of us burst out laughing.

We travel to Jiujiang prefecture and pay our respects at monasteries[148] founded by Chan patriarchs.

Presently, we arrived at Xilin[149] Temple to pay our respects. There, we spent the night.

The next day, we went to Jiujiang prefecture. The sun was already sinking in the west when we arrived. Residents of the hermitages that were located outside the city wall refused to admit guests, telling us that throughout the area, giving lodgings to outsiders was strictly prohibited.[150] We were told that guest accommodations were to be had across the river.

---

147. In her article "Violence and Political Protest in Ming and Qing China," Harriet Zurndorfer notes the necessity for "(p)aramilitary organizations, anti-bandit crop-watching corps" and other local vigilante activities in response to late-Ming political chaos in these areas. Harriet T. Zurndorfer. 1983. "Violence and Political Protest in Ming and Qing China." *International Review of Social History* 28 (3): 312. https://www.jstor.org/stable/44583728

148. *daochang* (*bodhi-maṇḍa*, Skt.)

149. Western Forest Temple

150. another example of public wariness during uncertain times

The Rambling Story of a Dream

There was nothing for it but endure the pangs of hunger and cross the river. Once our boat had reached the middle of the river, the boatman demanded payment. I untied my legging bands and handed them over to him. Among the other passengers was a Daoist who noticed this exchange. He paid our fares himself.

Once we had reached the opposite shore, we asked the people next to us where we could stay for the night, only to be told that no lodgings were available in that vicinity; likewise, there was no Buddhist hermitage nearby. They advised us to follow the river embankment for seventy *li*[151] to Zaogang,[152] where we would find a place called Wuzu Limu Dun.[153] There, we would find a small Buddhist hermitage that offered tea to visitors and received monks.

Hearing that, I told Chengzhuo and Juexin, "We've been tricked. That monastic teahouse is far away and the southwest wind is blowing hard, but we'll have to forge ahead as quickly as possible. There's no point in hanging around here."

Covering our mouths and faces, the three of us braved the fierce gale and set off quickly under the moon. It was after midnight when we reached our destination. We knocked on the door to request lodgings. Fortunately, the head of the hermitage was a monastic of compassion and *bodhicitta*.[154] Hearing our knock, he immediately got up, opened the door, and invited us in. He wondered what had brought us out in the middle of the night, so we

---

151. around 22 miles

152. Chisel Harbor

153. the pier where the Fifth Patriarch took leave of his mother to become a monk

154. the enlightenment mind devoted to the benefit all sentient beings

Jiujiang prefecture

gave him a detailed account of our recent misadventures. Hearing our tale, he heaved a long sigh, deeply lamenting the bitter experiences that befell foot travelers. Then, he happily brewed us some tea.

Admiring his great hospitality, I told him, "If we hadn't been refused admittance to the temples of Jiujiang, this demonstration of Way-mind[155] would never have occurred!"

The next day after breakfast, we asked the head monastic about the route that lay before us. He explained that in the past, every ancestral hall and temple precinct along our route had fallen into a state of decay. Fortunately, the Monk Sanmei had had everything rethatched and restored to its original condition.

Our group accordingly decided to visit these Buddhist sites and pay homage.[156] We set off for Huangmei county,[157] ascended Po'e Mountain, worshipped at the monastery founded by the fourth Chan patriarch, and then arrived again at Mount Fengmao, where we paid homage at the monastery founded by the fifth Chan patriarch.[158] We visited Gaoshan Temple,[159] worshipped at the monastery of Patriarch Jingjian, passed through Lingdangling to reach an ancient temple, and made obeisance at the monastery of Patriarch Qiansui Baozhang.[160] After that, we went to

---

155. *saṃbodhyamāna* [Skt]

156. Buddhists attained merit by visiting temples. At each location, their ordination certificates or yearbooks were stamped. The three travellers, who were still novices, presumably carried refuge or tonsure certificates.

157. Yellow Plum county in Hubei.

158. Hongren (601–674 CE)

159. 'High Mountain'

160. Qiansui Baozhang (414 BCE–657 CE) is so named because he lived for over a thousand years and was born with both hands tightly clasped in fists. His hands only opened after he took his *śrāmaṇera* vows at the age of nine. He was an Indian monk born into the Brahman caste. Qiansui deeply lamented having been

The Rambling Story of a Dream

Qianshan county and worshipped at the monastery of the Third Patriarch.[161] Next, we reached Qingyang county[162] and made a pilgrimage to Mount Jiuhua.[163]

Looking down from the main temple hall, we noticed a hermitage, so we went there to register[164] for the night. The hermitage didn't provide us with an evening meal. The next morning, our group sat around for quite some time waiting for breakfast to be served. Finally, the head monastic came out and explained that the monastery didn't have the financial resources to provide vegetarian meals for guests—it could only provide lodging. He suggested that we go to a family residence and beg for a meal.

At this, I told my two companions, "A family residence won't have a vegetarian kitchen. How could they possibly give us pure food? Let's go somewhere else!"

We went immediately to the temple's main hall and worshipped the Buddha image, and then we descended the mountain on empty stomachs. After walking for over ten *li*, we reached a hermitage, where we finally got a little bit to eat.

At Taiping prefecture

When we reached Taiping prefecture, we heard that Dharma Master Rongwu was giving a seminar on the Lotus Sūtra at Qingshan Temple, which was not far away from the

---

born over 90 years after the Buddha entered *Mahaparinirvana*. The saint's entire life was devoted to rigorous spiritual practice.

161. Jianzhi Sengcan (496?–606 CE)

162. in southern Anhui province

163. Nine-Flower Mountain: one of the four holy mountains for Chinese Buddhists

164. Wandering monastics had to show their Buddhist documentation and be approved by the guest prefect in order to be allowed to stay in the *yunshui* hall.

prefecture. Delighted, we asked for directions to the temple and set out.

By the time we arrived at the temple, the sun was already sinking among the hills. When the business office manager[165] saw our plain staves, wide-brimmed bamboo hats, and reed cushions, he refused to let us register as guests. We pleaded with him for admittance. Seeing that the hour was late and travel would be difficult, he ordered someone to lead us outside the monastery gate to a small Tudi shrine,[166] where we could pass the night. At the little shrine, we spread out our mats and saluted one another. We then sat down face to face.

I told the group, "Since we've come to learn about the Dharma, how can we possibly go back without fulfilling our mission?"

The following morning, we returned to the temple, where we had a breakfast of congee and listened to a sūtra lecture. Afterwards, we trekked back down the mountain, begging the local folk that we encountered for food and travel directions. Thus, we continued on our journey.

We reach Nanjing.

At around ten o'clock in the morning, on the tenth day of the lunar month, we came to Nanjing. Far off in the distance, we could see the lofty tower of the Bao'en Temple.[167] Its multi-

---

165. *dangjia seng*

166. Tudi is the local deity in charge of a locality's ground and soil.

167. The Porcelain Tower of Nanjing, designed during the reign of the Yongle Emperor (r. 1402–1424), was part of the Great Bao'en Temple. In its time, it was one of the tallest buildings in China. Europeans who visited Nanjing in the 17th and 18th centuries considered this pagoda to be one of the seven wonders of the world. It was constructed as the repository for a relic of the Buddha's cranium; the Tripitaka Hall in the southern temple precinct houses a relic of the parietal bone of the famous Tang-dynasty monk Xuanzang.

colored Buddhist radiance soared up into the sky, sparkling in the sunlight.

We entered the temple precincts and prostrated ourselves reverently; then, we walked around the great tower. By noon, our stomachs were empty. We asked some worshippers at the tower where a refectory was to be found that offered vegetarian fare to visiting monks.

One person pointed to the Tripitaka Hall in the south temple corridor: "That's the place."

We went there and paid reverence to the Buddha. Once we had made obeisance, we waited next to the temple stairs. Monks were entering and leaving the hall, but no one paid any attention to us. The three of us had no idea what the problem might be. We got up and left. Outside the temple precincts, we met an elderly monk and asked him what was going on.

He told us, "Nanjing boasts a renowned lecture center and meditation hall. If your shoes and clothing are tidy and orderly, if you are in harmony with the Chan order and are a pure guest, someone will come out and receive you. You are only itinerant monks out on a pilgrimage: people won't bother with scruffy monks like you."

If you aren't part of the saṃgha, you are not welcome in our midst.

After hearing the monk's words, we entered the city and arrived at the drum and bell towers[168] of the Western Great Buddha hermitage, where we registered as wandering monks. The hermitage didn't have a Buddha hall;

---

168. Drum and bell towers flank a gatehouse, respectively on the left and right sides.

instead, only a reed mat canopy had been placed above the Buddha image.

The head of the hermitage was a true spiritual practitioner. Here, all monastic guests were offered meals, and we were welcomed with joyful cordiality.

Upon learning that we came from Yun'nan, our host suggested, "The business office manager[169] of the Nanjing Xingshan Temple is also from Yun'nan. His ordination name is Yinwu. Why don't you go there and pay him a call? He'll assuredly offer you accommodation."

The next day at noon, we went there to register. We noticed that the itinerant saṃgha was given stale, verminous rice to eat accompanied by a vegetable dish consisting of stinky, poorly-salted Chinese scallions or some such fare. We entered the dormitory and then toured the monastery, only to find that the long-term monastery residents dined upon fresh vegetables served with clean white rice.

Kuoran, a disciple of the head manager, was also from Yun'nan and recognized our accent. That evening, he came to the hall for itinerant monks to visit with us, his fellow townsfolk. I explained that we were from Guizhou.[170] He continued to probe us with questions, making a laborious effort to decide whether or not we were respectable enough to be allowed to stay there as resident monks.

I observed to Chengzhuo and Juexin: "We've come on such a long, challenging journey with profound dedication—we should place our reliance upon virtuous spiritual friends,[171] rather than tolerate a mean-spirited person like this who is blind to sincere devotion. He has no consid-

---

169. *dangjia*
170. Guizhou is contiguous with Yun'nan on its western border.
171. kalyāṇamitra [Skt]

eration for others. We should willingly abide in honest poverty rather than demean ourselves by accepting his grudging favors. It is not appropriate to become familiar with such a person."

Monastic deportment

Upon hearing that Master Juewu was lecturing on the Śūraṃgama Sūtra at the Yuanjue hermitage, we went out through the city gate to attend.

When we arrived at the hermitage, we met charitable lay Buddhists who provided vegetarian fare for the monks. Travelling monastics from the ten directions were seated on the floor of Skanda Hall. For every two people, four wooden dishes of vegetables were provided. During the meal, I was paired with an itinerant monk. It was my practice to maintain correct monastic deportment by taking food slowly; however, my partner's chopsticks kept on moving relentlessly until he had scarfed down all four plates of food.

After the meal, I went out and told my two comrades, "After this, if our karma leads us to offer vegetarian food to others, we should pile every entrée—no matter how many individual dishes there may be—into a single large bowl and let everyone eat together. First of all, in the presence of so many others, each diner will have to pay more attention to proper monastic decorum; secondly, a shared meal will foster mutual trust and respect.

"The monk that I sat with today was entirely undisciplined. He ate ravenously: his manners were no different than those of a starving person!"

Two people cannot register together.

We also went to the Pude Temple to participate in ceremonies and do some sightseeing. We entered the meditation hall and registered as visiting monks. That evening, we discussed our plans. The tenth lunar month was now drawing to a close and the weather was too frigid for foot travel. It would be better to stay at the temple for the time being and continue our journey in the warmth of spring. The next morning, after eating our breakfast congee, we applied to the prior for a period of residency.

His reply was, "Name cards for assigned seating[172] cannot be issued for two people together, and certainly not for a party of three.

Looking me over, he continued, "But I'll allot you a place. You can serve as the verger[173] and attend to the incense and lanterns; you'll stay in the incense board hall."[174]

I laughed at this suggestion, telling him, "I am far too clumsy to manage raising a wick in a glass oil lamp."

Thus, the three of us packed our luggage and strode out through the monastery gates.

I told Chengzhuo and Juexin, "Since monasteries in the capital city refuse to register three people together, we'd best separate temporarily for the winter and arrange to meet again on the thirtieth day of the twelfth lunar month. I've

---

172. Monastics were assigned places on platforms in a temple training hall, with name cards to mark each space.

173. *xiangdengshi*

174. *xiangbantang*: "Incense" boards were paddles that were used to keep the meditation monks alert. The instructor, abbot, and meditation patrol each carried a different type of board, that was held at a prescribed angle. Holmes Welch, *The Practice of Chinese Buddhism,* 1900–1950 (Cambridge: Harvard University Press, 1973) 66–7. https://terebess.hu/zen/mesterek/Holmes-Welch-The-Practice.pdf

heard that on Baohua Mountain, they specialize in teaching the sūtras. I'd like to make a thorough study of the Śūraṃgama mantra there."

Chengzhuo said, "Juexin and I will stay at Zutang Mountain.[175] Once you've learned the Śūraṃgama mantra, you can meet us there."

I exchanged my meditation cushion for Juexin's bedding, and then we went our separate ways.

I ascend Baohua Mountain.

By the time I had climbed halfway up the mountain slope, the sun had already set among the hills. I lodged at the Shimen hermitage.

That evening at teatime, I told the head of the hermitage my plan: "I've heard that those on Mount Baohua place great importance upon sūtra study and teaching. My intention is to go there."

The head monastic replied, "There's a retired head seat monk living at Baohua. He's from Yun'nan and has spent a considerable amount of time in the northern capital. This monk came to Baohua Mountain ten years ago. He's read the entire Buddhist canon three times over and takes great delight in diligent students. I, too, have studied sūtras under his tutelage.

"Very few people live at the temple, which only has four house heads.[176] Fortunately, everyone is served from one pot of food—there are no separate rice and vegetable

---

175. 'Mountain' signified a Buddhist temple. The Zutang (patriarchs' hall) mountains lie in the Nanjing area.

176. *fangtou*

dishes.[177] Wandering monks on a pilgrimage to the bronze hall are always given lodging and food, even though the three daily meals consist only of thin gruel.

"Since your intention is to live on the mountain and pursue Buddhist studies, you should cast aside the aggregates[178] of your physical body, habitual thoughts, and feelings: don't be put off by the temple's honest poverty."

A man of character does not partake of food of questionable provenance.

The next morning, I ascended the mountain and reached the monastery precincts, which were managed by resident monks. After worshipping the Buddha image, I spent the rest of the day touring the temple and paying my respects to the monks living there. I experienced an indistinct sense of *déjà vu*: everything seemed oddly familiar, as though I had been there before.

I paid the head seat[179] monk a formal visit. After prostrating myself, I explained that my intention was to study the Śūraṃgama mantra.

The master inquired, "Where is your hometown? How long have you been a monk? To study this mantra, you must prepare beforehand and learn the entire text by heart."

I replied that I was from Yun'nan and had only recently gone forth and become a monk. As soon as I'd taken my vows, I had come to Jiang'nan. I hadn't read the text because I couldn't understand the words.

---

177. Standard temple fare consisted of a bowl of rice or congee accompanied by a bowl of salted or pickled vegetables.

178. The five aggregates are the direct fruits of our previous lives.

179. rector: the leader of the front hall class.

The Rambling Story of a Dream

The master granted my request, saying, "Since you have come to these mountains, you can serve as a waiter.[180] You will live in the kitchen."

By the eleventh lunar month, the weather was frigid and the ground frozen. After washing and stacking the dishes, they would all freeze together and become hard to separate. To prevent the clean dishes from freezing together, I wiped them dry with a clean piece of cloth. That way, when they were needed the next day, they would separate easily. The person assigned to bring buckets of water on a carrying pole didn't have time to get the job done, so I chipped in and carried water myself.

Liaoran was the head cook's[181] Dharma name. He was young and clever. There was also an official who supervised the business office staff.[182] Every day, he would measure out grains and produce that were kept in the storehouse, and then hand them over to the head cook, who would use the daily allotment for cooking rice and vegetable dishes. As soon as the head cook got these supplies, he would set aside a portion for himself.

One day, when I came back from a Śūraṃgama mantra memorization lesson, he invited me to eat some of the cooked rice that he had kept for himself.

I asked him, "Where did this firm cooked rice come from? Everyone in the temple only gets thin rice porridge."

He replied, "I have set this aside for you with kindly intentions, yet you react by cross-examining me!"

I retorted, "How can an honorable person eat food of uncertain provenance?!"

---

180. *xingtang*: Kitchen duty would involve performing odd jobs like dishwashing and serving meals.
181. *dianzuo*
182. *fangtou*

Food of questionable provenance

Saying this, I got up and left the room.

After that incident, all of the kitchen staff went on the defensive, forming a clique to shield one another from scrutiny. They no longer wanted me living in their midst. The head cook had a secret conference with the prior.[183] There was no one assigned to the timekeeper's hall, so I was sent to live in the room where the wooden boards were kept. There, I would be in charge of keeping time for temple activities by burning sticks of incense and striking a board as a signal to the monastery.[184]

The timekeeper's hall was spacious and empty, and the bed was quite large. Sleeping there alone was like lying in an ice house. There was an elderly hall head[185] with the ordination name Yunshan[186] who had formerly been a court eunuch. He was a sincere seeker of the Way; his heart was imbued with compassion and bodhicitta. He'd seen how I maintained my lofty intentions and kept my vow of poverty. Deep in the night, he pushed open the door where I was staying and entered.

Close to my ear, he whispered: "Here's something to help protect you from the cold!"

As soon as he said this, he left the room. I reached out and felt what he'd brought: it resembled cotton batting but wasn't soft to the touch. Although it covered my body, it

---

183. *douguan*

184. Monasteries had no clocks for timekeeping; rather, every activity was timed by burning sticks of incense. The length of time that a specific incense stick took to burn was used to time Chan practice sessions. Even the night watchman timed his rounds by burning incense. Boards were struck to announce temple activities. The intricate daily schedule of a large monastery was regulated by boards, bells, chimes, a wooden fish, drums, and chimes.

185. *fangtou*

186. Cloud Mountain

The Rambling Story of a Dream

wasn't at all warm. When daylight came, I saw that the bed was covered with a patchwork of old cotton batting. Although it was a miserable gift, I was still deeply grateful to the monk for his kindness and compassion.[187]

By the sixteenth day of the twelfth lunar month, I had completed my study of the Śūraṃgama mantra. I went respectfully to the head seat master to convey my thanks.

The master told me, "On the first day of the New Year, a lay Buddhist named Sang from Hekouzhen[188] will be coming to this temple to participate in the repentance rite of Emperor Wu of the Liang dynasty.[189] You have completed your study of the mantra, a rare achievement. If you stay here for the repentance ceremony, almsgivers will provide you with new shoes, clothing, and monastic equipment."[190]

But I'd already arranged to rejoin Chengzhuo and Juexin on that day, so I wasn't interested in staying on for the assembly. At daybreak on the twenty-eighth day of the twelfth lunar month, I arose and made three prostrations in the direction of the head seat master's quarters, and then turned around and went back down the mountain.

When I reached Dongyang,[191] I asked for directions to the Zutang mountains. Then, I traveled over a hundred *li* [192] to reach my destination. By the time I arrived, the sun

---

187. *karuṇā*

188. a province in Yun'nan

189. Emperor Wu of the Liang dynasty (464–549 CE) was a devout Buddhist who implemented many Buddhist ideals in his policies. He composed this repentance ceremony for his deceased wife, who had appeared to him in a dream lamenting her evil deeds. Such rituals are enacted to gain merit and free participants from karmic bondage.

190. Great merit is acquired by giving alms to arhats and Buddhist monastics.

191. in modern Zhejiang province

192. around 31 miles

had set and a myriad of stars twinkled in the night sky. At the mountain temple, I asked about the whereabouts of Chengzhuo and Juexin.

The monk in charge of the hall for itinerant monks told me, "A few days ago, those two went off on a pilgrimage to Nanhai.[193] Just before leaving, they left a message: 'If Shaoru of Mount Hua comes looking for us, tell him to follow us and meet us along the road.'"

I set off early the next day. While trekking through Oxhead village, I happened to run into the Dharma propagator Dunxiu. We had previously met at the Shuiyue hermitage in Guizhou. He insisted upon keeping me there to pass the New Year holiday. The next day, I had a bite to eat and left without announcing my departure.

I arrived at the Ling'gu Temple in Nanjing on the thirtieth day of the twelfth lunar month.[194] There was a motley group of roistering monks staying in the yunshui dormitory; the place was aquake with din and commotion. There was no space for me to settle down for the night, so I huddled behind the door and sat there until dawn. I had rice congee for breakfast, and then continued on my way.

As soon as I got outside, I ran into the monk in charge of donations,[195] whose ordination name was Hongchuan.

He told me cordially, "Today is New Year's Day—why are you leaving? Please go back in and take it easy for a few days!"

He showed such sincere understanding of the Buddha path[196] that I acceded to his request and went back into

---

193. They were now in Jiangsu province, which abuts the South China Sea (Nanhai).

194. Jianyue was thirty-four years old. It was the eighth Chongzhen regnal year.

195. *huazhu*: This title might imply either a teaching leader (*jiaohua zhu*) or a donations official.

196. *jñāna*

the temple. After eating a vegetarian lunch, I again left the Ling'gu Temple. I walked twenty *li* [197] and spent the night at a small hermitage.

Begging for ordination at Gulin[198] hermitage

On the second day of the new year, I stopped for a rest at the Tuqiao south hermitage.[199] On the third day of the lunar new year, while continuing my journey, I suddenly ran into Chengzhuo, who was walking towards me from the opposite direction.

I asked him what had happened: "The two of you went on a pilgrimage to Nanhai together. Why are you coming back alone?"

He replied, "Juexin got to Wuxi[200] and wanted to continue his pilgrimage to the seacoast. Afterwards, I went to Hangzhou and heard that the old monk Sanmei was at Jiululing[201] on Mount Wutai promulgating the great precepts. I came back looking for you so that we can go there together."

Hearing this, I returned, "Mount Wutai is extremely far away, and there is no way of verifying what you have heard. Let's go to the Gulin hermitage in Nanjing and receive the precepts there. The Gulin hermitage was founded by the monk Guxin, the patriarch of the Vinaya school of Buddhism.[202] How about it?"

---

197. six or seven miles

198. Ancient Forest

199. in modern Hunan province

200. Their pilgrimage might have included the Southern Chan Temple (*Nanchan si*) in Wuxi.

201. in modern Shanxi province

202. Gulin (Ancient Forest) (1541–1615) was the Buddhist courtesy name of Ruxing, who founded the Gulin school of Buddhism.

Begging for ordination

Thus, the two of us went to the Gulin hermitage, where we asked to receive the precepts. The hermitage guest master told us that in order to be ordained, we'd have to pay a registration fee of one silver tael and five mace in addition to furnishing our own robes and bowls.

As it happened, Chengzhuo had monastic robes but no money, while I had neither robes nor money. I did have an amber rosary[203] from Dami Village in Yun'nan, however. I handed my prayer beads over to the guest master in lieu of payment for my robes and registration.

Apparently acquiescing to this arrangement, he took the rosary, turned around, and went back inside. My eyesight and hearing are quite keen, so I knew what was happening inside the building.

I perceived someone peering at us furtively from a window and heard someone inside the hermitage say, "Those two are just wandering rogues, and who knows how they came by that rosary. Those prayer beads are probably ill-gotten gain. Don't let them register."

After their consultation, the guest master came back out and told us, "It is not possible for us to process such a request. Procure the necessary funds and equipment, and then come back and try again!"

Taking back my rosary, I turned around to leave.

The guest master invited us to take a meal before departing, but I replied, "A dragon must return to the great ocean—how can it possibly stay trapped in a cramped cow-hoof den like this!"

We left the temple immediately and found another hermitage, where we passed the night. The next day, we crossed the Yangtze River and reached Pukou.[204]

---

203. *mālā* [Skt]
204. in Nanjing

The Rambling Story of a Dream

On the road to Wutai Mountain

On the fourteenth day of the first lunar month, we lodged in Hongxinpu. Rumors were abroad that rampaging bands of rebels were approaching. There was widespread wailing and outcry among the inhabitants, both male and female. Children were abandoned in a frantic scramble to flee the coming storm. The wretchedness and brutality were unspeakable.[205]

Chengzhuo and I had neither consumed a drop of water nor a grain of rice that entire day; we were famished. We fled along the road from morning to dusk, covered over a hundred *li*, and lodged at Sanpu that evening. On the night of the fifteenth, rebel bands broke through the city wall of Fengyang and burned down the imperial mausoleum. Chengzuo and I went north until we reached Xuzhou,[206] where we finally had a chance to rest.

The next day, we wanted to cross the Yellow River. There were no boats, so we just sat on the riverbank awaiting transportation. We waited there until noon, when a troop of mounted imperial messengers came by. They seized a boatman and his boat, and we crossed the river with them. When we got to the middle of the river, the currents became turbulent. The boatman was drunk and his hands were slack; to make matters worse, the boat was old, worn-out, and leaky. The imperial messengers were in a panic, loudly imploring heaven to save them. Chengzhuo and I just concentrated single-mindedly on chanting the Buddha's

---

205. It has been speculated that a million people were massacred in these late-Ming uprisings.

206. In modern Jiangsu province. Xuzhou was an important center for the imperial courier and grain tribute systems.

name. Fortunately, a gentle breeze arose and wafted the boat into a thicket of rushes, where it came to rest in the shallows. The two of us grabbed onto the rushes, waded through the water, and went ashore. That night, we lodged at a derelict hermitage.

Paying our respects to the elderly Monk Sanmei

The following day, our long-distance trek began in earnest. Sometimes, we would brave the wind and rain; sometimes, we journeyed under the moon and stars. We'd beg for food at villages or from farmers that we met along the way.

On the first day of the third lunar month, we reached Changchengkou. We crossed through Longquan pass,[207] set foot on the Shanxi border, and finally reached the Jiululing Temple of Mount Wutai. The temple hall for visiting monks was located outside the monastery proper. As soon as Chengzhuo and I had registered and settled our belongings, we went to the abbot's quarters to pay our respects to the elderly Monk Sanmei.

Two monks from northern China were on duty at the door.

One of them told us, "If you give us an 'incense donation,' we'll give you leave to enter; otherwise, buzz off."

His tone was coarse and gruff; we saw immediately that there was no way to reason with him. There was nothing to be done but turn around and go back to the guest house.

With a long sigh of disappointment, I said, "We've climbed mountains and forded rivers, never regarding a thousand-*li* journey as excessive. Our goal has been to meet

---

207. Dragon Spring Pass, in modern Hebei province

spiritual friends, yet we've been turned away at the door for not paying a gratuity. What's to be done?"

Chengzhuo replied, "There's no need to get frustrated. Tomorrow morning when the doormen have gone to eat their breakfast porridge, we'll just enter the abbot's quarters and pay our respects."

Early the next day, enduring hunger pangs, we went straight to the abbot's room and paid our respects to the Monk.

"Where have you two come from?" he asked us curtly.

"We've come from Yun'nan," I answered.

"Why have you come here?" the Monk pursued.

Since we had neither robes nor bowls, we didn't dare to broach the topic of ordination; instead, we told him that we had come to visit Mount Wutai.

At this, the Monk replied, "The bodhisattva Mañjuśrī[208] resides where you came from, yet you two have come on a misguided pilgrimage to Mount Wutai. Assiduously chant the Buddha's name and refine your spiritual practice!"

We hastily made obeisance to the elderly monk and took our leave with thanks for his advice. Once outside, we vowed that someday, if we became qualified to act as spiritual friends, we would never require gifts from visiting monks, so that penniless monastics would be able to obtain an audience with us easily.

Sūtra-reading by lamplight

Following this encounter, we ascended the mountain and reached Tayuan Temple.[209] There were two supervisors at

---

208. Mount Wutai is a center for the worship of Mañjuśrī, the bodhisattva of wisdom.

209. a prominent Chan temple in Shanxi province

Sūtra-reading by lamplight

the temple, both disciples of the same master, who had earnestly resolved to intone five great Mahāyāna sūtras[210] in a three-year period. They inquired about our background. Once they found out that we had journeyed all the way from Yun'nan, they were impressed and delightedly allowed us to stay there.

Chengzhuo volunteered to provide the temple with water by serving as a water-bearer, allowing me to enter the temple hall for sūtra-chanting. When Chengzhuo's work was done, he concentrated on studying the Lotus Sūtra. Apart from entering the Dharma hall to participate in worship services, my remaining spare time was spent reading the Śūraṃgama sūtra yi hai.[211]

At the temple, Chengzhuo and I never indulged in idle conversation, nor did we do any casual running around; we were unflaggingly busy every day, never resting until the middle of the night.

Every temple and shrine on Mount Wutai, whether large or small, used oat flour mixed into a paste for porridge. The abbot of the Tayuan Temple had the ordination name Deyun. He, as well as the hall managers[212] and saṃgha members, noticed how diligently we were working. For over a month, we hadn't altered our strict regime by a hair. To demonstrate their trust and respect, they took us aside and offered us rice porridge to eat.

---

210. *Dafang guangfo huayan jing* (*Mahā-vaipulya-buddhâvataṃsaka-sūtra*); *Dabo niepan jing* (*Mahāparinirvāṇa sūtra*); *Jinguangming jing* (*Suvarṇaprabhāsottama sūtra*); *Da fangbian fo bao'en jing* (*The Great Skillful Means Sūtra on the Buddha's Repayment of Kindness*: Scholars suspect that this text is of Chinese provenance.); *Dacheng benxing xindi guan jing* (*Mūlajāta-hṛidayabhūmi-dhyāna-sūtra*).

211. "The Ocean of Meaning in the Śūraṃgama Sūtra"

212. *fangtou*

Chengzhuo and I talked things over: "The two of us have been studying until late at night in the midst of all the other monks, disrupting their sleep. If we go to the hall consecrated to the Dharma-protecting deities, we can light a glass lantern without bothering anybody. Let's go. No one is there, so studying by lamplight won't interfere with anyone's slumber. In the empty hall, we'll be able to focus our minds better on our studies; moreover, the silence will be conducive to memorization. We can study during the quiet hours of the night."

On Mount Wutai, the weather stays extremely cold during the spring and autumn seasons—imagine how frigid it is in the wintertime! It was now the tenth lunar month. Clad only in our flimsy robes, we held volumes of scriptures[213] in our hands and stood directly under the lamplight. We focused so assiduously upon our readings that we were oblivious to the cold. By the time we finally closed a volume to rest, our fingers were frozen stiff—we couldn't bend them. Our legs were so frozen and numb that we could barely walk, our bodies shook and trembled, the intense cold had penetrated our internal organs. But rather than deter us from continuing our nightly studies, this hardship only strengthened our resolve.

My first time mounting the lecture podium

Spring ushered in the ninth year of the Chongzhen regnal era.[214] At the end of the second lunar month, Juexin returned

---

213. By the Ming dynasty, scriptures were printed from woodblocks and kept in special cases.

214. 1636. The Chongzhen emperor, Zhu Youjian, inherited the imperial throne when the Ming empire was in a state of disintegration due to

Mounting the lecture podium

to Nanjing from his coastal pilgrimage. He had continued to ask about our whereabouts along the way back and finally rejoined us on Mount Wutai.

In the middle of the third lunar month, a monk came to Wutai on a pilgrimage. He was from Hubei; his ordination name was Jiaoru. As it happened, we had both been at Baoqing prefecture to attend Grandmaster Zhuanyu's seminar on the four types of reliance expounded in the Śūraṃgama Sūtra. He caught sight of us in the temple hall and came over to greet us. The people around us were curious as to how we had become acquainted, so he reported on my wanderings in great detail.

Upon hearing his recital of my activities, the abbot, Master Deyun, arranged a vegetarian banquet and called together every temple monastic to partake. In addition, he requested that I give a seminar on the Śūraṃgama Sūtra starting on the first day of the fourth lunar month. I was deeply grateful for the evident esteem in which I was held, but rueful that there was no way to shirk the responsibility of lecturing at the assembly. I could think of no way out and had to agree to the proposal. On the first day of the seventh lunar month, the retreat came to a close.

It was the first time that my two companions and I had visited Mount Wutai; so far, we had stayed exclusively at the Tayuan Temple. Since we hadn't yet paid our respects at the other Buddhist temples on the five peaks, we set off

---

corrupt officials and palace eunuchs who had been exploiting the populace mercilessly.

Zhu's mighty efforts to reform the government were eventually thwarted due to a torrent of setbacks: numerous rebellions, Manchu raiders from northeast China, severe natural disasters, economic depression, and widespread unemployment. When rebel groups led by Li Zicheng invaded Beijing in the spring of 1644, the emperor abdicated and committed suicide.

for Dongtai Peak[215] on the third day of the seventh lunar month. The temple's chief monk[216] met us with the ceremonious hospitality shown to Dharma masters. After our visit to Dongtai Peak, we proceeded to Beitai, the northern peak, where the business office manager[217] received us with the same lavish courtesy. Such treatment caused me to feel uneasy and embarrassed. To avoid further awkwardness, we didn't visit the other peaks.

Going to Beijing

On the eighth day of the month, we formally took our leave of the Tayuan Temple's abbot, as well as the monastics from every part of the temple precincts.[218] We planned on going to Beijing and requesting full ordination from the monk Sanmei. Reluctant to let us go, the abbot and masters tried earnestly to persuade us to stay at the temple. When they realized that our hearts were set upon leaving, they readied three mules for us, and saw Juexin, Chengzhuo, and me off. Members of the temple escorted us all the way back to Jiululing, where the entire party passed the night. The next morning, Master Deyun was still unwilling to part with us. He continued to accompany us to Shuxiayuan[219] in Tangli Village.[220] The next morning, he treated us to a vegetarian meal, and then bade farewell to each one of us individually. When he was saying his last good-byes, his eyes brimmed with tears.

---

215. the eastern peak

216. *zhuchi seng*

217. *dangjia seng*

218. The temple currently has 130 buildings, including temple halls and dormitories.

219. "Courtyard under the trees"

220. Birchleaf Pear Village: Several Chinese villages bear this name.

Finally, he entreated us: "Once you've received the full precepts, please come back to Wutai. Don't let us down and dash our fervent hopes."

We arrive in Baoding.

On the nineteenth day of the seventh lunar month, we arrived at western Fangshunqiao Town in Baoding prefecture.[221] We spent the night at the Luohou Temple.[222]

During our stay on Mount Wutai, Chengzhuo had made the acquaintance of a certain Daoist. They had arranged to meet in Cangzhou,[223] so he set off to keep the rendezvous.

The next day in the afternoon, Juexin and I left the temple to go hiking with six other people. Far off in the distance, we saw a grove of trees. With its deep green foliage, the spot looked invitingly shady, so we decided to go there. Enjoying the refreshing coolness, we sat for rather a long time, until the sun was about to set.

We were just about to get up and return to the temple, when we noticed a patch of dusky grey looming in the sky: it looked like fog. Along with this apparition, we heard volleys of confused, agitated noises. Gradually, the soaring patch of dust shifted like a cloud, and we began to see countless men and women, both old and young, running wildly all over the countryside. Like a landslide or tsunami, the crowd surged towards us. We then realized that these people were being attacked by pursuing soldiers.

All of our fellow hikers made a run for it, scattering in different directions. Only Juexin and I remained under the

---

221. in modern Hebei province
222. This temple was named after Rāhula, the Buddha's only son.
223. a city in Hebei

trees. There was no question of going back to the temple now. We didn't dare to take any main roads. In a panic, we fled towards the south. For the most part, we took shelter in small shrines that we came upon along the way. Every day, we only ate a single meal.

I change my Buddhist name to Jianyue.

During our headlong flight from danger, we waded through ditches, got lost, and took random detours. On the road one day, our hunger pangs were so sharp that we had to rest under a tree next to a desolate tomb.

I observed to Juexin: "We started off from Yun'nan and went south, and then we travelled from the south of China to the north. Now, here we are again going from north to south. We've gone back and forth, covering over 20,000 li. We've trudged all over in vain, never fulfilling our vow.

"The Buddhist master who shaved my head gave me the ordination name Shaoru[224] because he hoped that I would propagate the Dharma and benefit all sentient beings. But the way things are going, it looks like that karmic thread has been severed—how shameful!

"My Dharma name is Duti.[225] The character *ti* means 'body'—the Dharma-body[226] that has absolute existence, the fundamental substance of all things, ultimate emptiness. The character *du* means 'to read.' Therefore, my name implies studying the Buddhist scriptures until one arrives at a complete understanding of the contents expounded

---

224. The name implies carrying on a tradition.
225. The characters for Duti signify 'read' and 'body,' from which the convoluted logical sequence above is derived.
226. *dharmakāya* [Skt]

I change my Buddhist name to Jianyue

therein. When these fundamental principles are understood, there is no further need for written exposition or clarification. It's just like a finger pointing at the moon: once you see the moon, you have no further need of that pointing finger to guide your eyes. I am now going to change my courtesy name to Jianyue—'seeing the moon.'"

But now, what were we to do? The two of us cudgeled our brains; the more we considered our situation, the more sorrowful we felt. So heartbroken were we that bitter tears trickled down our cheeks unheeded and unchecked.

Just then, an old man happened to pass by. He saw that we were in a wretched state and came over to find out what was the matter. I explained our miserable plight to him in detail: how we had journeyed on foot over an immense distance yet had been unable to achieve our goal. The old man sighed repeatedly as he listened to our story.

Finally, he said, "My surname is Li. I am a Daoist and have been a vegetarian for many years. I have no family and live alone. Usually, I make a living by tutoring people's children, but now that the country is in a state of chaos, I've come back home. I live in the village just a little way up the road from here. You can pass the night with me before setting off again on your journey."

When we got to his house, we saw that it had already been looted by rebel thieves, who had left nothing behind. Our host borrowed some coarse flour from his next-door neighbor and made us grilled pancakes. The next day, we said goodbye to him and continued on our way.

The Rambling Story of a Dream

We encounter an elderly monk on the road to Nangong county.[227]

We kept on travelling for six days, and then got on the main road to Nangong county. It was now afternoon, and we had yet to come across a place where we could beg for food. Far off in the distance, we saw a small hermitage. When we got there, I went inside the hermitage alone, while Juexin remained outside.

In the hermitage, there was only one elderly monk with nobody there to help him. The monk was boiling a pot of rice. I joined my palms respectfully and inquired about his situation; he didn't return my salutation. I came over and helped him to prepare the meal. When the rice was done, he filled a bowl, sat down, and started eating. I took a bowl and chopsticks and served myself rice, then sat down and started eating without saying a word. Once he had finished his first helping, I filled his bowl again.

Finally, he started talking: "I've never seen anyone like you before. The host doesn't say a word, yet you go unbidden and serve yourself rice."

I retorted, "I've never seen anyone like *you* before: a guest is standing right in front of you, but you never utter a single civil word, nor do you invite the guest to share your meal. That's why I went and helped myself."

He peered at me and started laughing, "Oh, it's a Chan monk. In my youth, I went travelling to visit and receive instruction from Buddhist masters. I wandered far and wide on foot, but due to my inexperience, I was always starving. It seems that you are in the same plight. Eat all you want!"

I told him that there was another Way-friend waiting outside the door. This news pleased the old monk.

---

227. located in southern Hebei province

"Invite him to come in and eat with us," he told me.

Juexin and I had a full meal, and then got up and bade our host farewell. The elderly monk wouldn't hear of our going and kept us there as his guests for three days.

Master Pingsu

At the beginning of the ninth lunar month, we reached Guazhou,[228] which is located in the Jiang'nan region south of the Yangtze River. There, we registered to stay at the Xilang hermitage.

We met a monk there from Yun'nan by the name of Qingru and got to talking about our travels. He, too, we discovered, had been in northern China, where he'd encountered rebel marauders and had been forced to flee back to the south. The next day, he joined our party of two when we went to cross the river. Our destination was the Ganlu Temple.[229]

The temple business manager,[230] whose Dharma name was Pingsu, was also from Yun'nan. He had spent many years in Zhenjiang prefecture, where he had made many converts to Buddhism. He took especial delight in welcoming his fellow provincials when they came to the Jiang'nan region to study and practise Buddhism.

When we got to the temple, Qingru entered first to announce us; Juexin and I went in afterwards and made our prostrations. Master Pingsu inquired about the perils that we had encountered on the road as foot travelers, and I gave him a straightforward account of the atrocities we'd seen without mincing words.

---

228. Guazhou means 'melon prefecture.'
229. the Sweet Dew Temple
230. *dangjia*

The Rambling Story of a Dream

He heard me out, and then pronounced calmly, "When I was young and out travelling in search of instruction from Buddhist masters, I also met with no little adversity, but that was no setback to my Way-seeking mind. And today, intersecting threads of causation have brought our paths together. The two of you have been journeying in search of a master who can transmit the precepts. You've gone back and forth from north to south; it has been a rough trip, but you've never slackened in your quest to fulfill your original intention.

"The karmic seeds that will enable you to guide and edify sentient beings were sown long ago and will naturally come to brilliant fruition. For the time being, just stay here. Rest assured that everything will work out."

"As it happens," he continued, "the first day of the lunar new year, the tenth year of the Chongzhen regnal era,[231] is the anniversary of that toilsome day on which my mother gave birth to me. In order to repay her great kindness, I want to intone five great scriptures. The two of you can chant the sūtras along with our saṃgha. I will make arrangements for your kāṣāya robes and ordination licenses.[232] Once the scripture recitation is over, you can continue on your way."

I replied, "The Monk Sanmei is far away in Beijing right now—we cannot go back there. We'll have to wait until he returns to the south before requesting ordination again. In the meantime, I'd like to go to the Tiantong Temple[233] to practise Chan meditation and seek spiritual instruction."

---

231. Master Jianyue was now 36 years old.

232. These government-issued licenses were obligatory for those who wanted to become monks or nuns. Ordination certificates were a lucrative source of income for the imperial coffers, since monasteries were often quite wealthy.

233. The "Heavenly Child" Temple is located on Mount Taibai in Zhejiang. It is one of the five prominent Chan temples in China.

The Haichao hermitage

Master Pingsu obligingly sponsored this trip. Besides purchasing luggage for us, he also gave us two taels, five mace each to defray our travel expenses.

Travelling from Danyang to the Haichao hermitage

On the third day of the second lunar month, we arrived at the Danyang county bridgehead. We wanted to cross the river on a passenger boat.

Setting our luggage down at his feet, Juexin was only paying attention to the boatmen, who were elbowing one another aside in fierce competition to pull in passengers. While he was watching this spectacle, our quilts, bags, and luggage were stolen. All that we could do was sigh over the karmic chain of cause and effect that had brought us to such a sorry pass!

Fortunately, my travel money was still hidden among my robes. By noon, we arrived at the Haihui hermitage and asked to register for a night's lodging, but when the residents saw that we had no luggage, they refused to assign us platform spaces. We explained that our luggage had been stolen on the bridgehead.

As it happened, the hermitage was located not far from the site of the robbery. Once the residents had verified our story, they escorted us to the hall where itinerant monks were given temporary accommodations.[234] There, we made the acquaintance of two roving monks. As it happened, we had spent several days travelling with these monks during our journey north.

When they learned that the two of us were foot travelers seeking ordination, they offered some timely advice: "So,

---

234. *yunshui tang*

The Rambling Story of a Dream

you want to receive the precepts. The Monk Sanmei has already left Beijing. In the first lunar month, he held an ordination at the Shita Temple[235] in Yangzhou prefecture. Right now, the Haichao hermitage[236] in Dantu county has requested him to officiate at an ordination ceremony. The proceedings will start on the eighth day of the second lunar month, so you'd better get moving straightaway if you want to undertake the precepts."

Upon hearing this news, the depression and gloom that had burdened our hearts so heavily dispersed like wisps of smoke.

Preceptor Xunliu

The next morning, Juexin and I turned around and went back to the Haichao hermitage. We arrived fortuitously just as the Monk Sanmei was being escorted inside.

We heard that the ordination preceptor,[237] whose Dharma name was Xunliu, was from the Chu region. He was magnanimous, wise, and clever. He guided and instructed novices with great dignity, taking charge of everything during the period set aside for the preparation and ordination of candidates. I asked the guest master to bring me to Xunliu's quarters so that I could make obeisance to him.

The monk asked where I was from, and I replied, "Yun'nan."

---

235. Stone Pagoda Temple

236. Tidewater hermitage

237. The Four-part Vinaya lists four different instructors (*ācāryas*) who are involved in the final ordination process. An ordination teacher performs the ceremony, a precept teacher explains monastic decorum and discipline, a karma instructor drills novices on the ordination ritual and recitations, and yet another instructor teaches scriptures. Temples weren't necessarily staffed with a full quota of teachers. Here, Xunliu seems to be the ritual and recitation drillmaster.

I relinquish my seating space

He then told me, "The business office manager has to pay for his master's burial promptly by the retreat's starting date: he is collecting one silver tael from each candidate. You must provide your own robes and alms-bowl."

I explained our situation: "All of our luggage was lost at Danyang. I myself am only carrying travel money amounting to two taels, three mace."

"That's just enough for one person's registration and contribution," he asserted. "It will also cover your robes and alms-bowl."

I then requested that my funds also be used to cover Juexin's registration fee. Once these arrangements were settled, someone was sent to escort me into the Vinaya study hall, while Juexin was taken to the refectory and assigned the task of waiting on diners during community meals.

I repeatedly give up my seating space to others.

The initiation master[238] in charge of the novice study hall was from Shandong; his ordination name was Eryuan. Although he was honest and straightforward, he lacked mental flexibility.

He was extremely displeased by my scanty equipment and dogged silence. I hadn't a scrap of luggage and never asked him for a Vinaya study manual. I would spend entire days upon my assigned platform space without uttering a word, yet I never violated any of the Vinaya hall rules. To make matters worse, I never had any questions to ask him.

---

238. *Yinlishi*: Several initiation masters might serve at the same ordination. They had the exacting duty of teaching and drilling novices. Like parents, they taught new monks how to eat, walk, make their beds, wrap up their travelling supplies, and so on. Additionally, they taught novices the gathas and mantras that had to be recited at precise times throughout the day.

Finally, he rebuked me, saying, "Jianyue, this is not a silent meditation space. Why haven't you requested a Vinaya study manual and started learning the contents by heart?"

My response was, "I cannot read the characters, nor do I have the money to purchase a Vinaya manual."

After that, every time an ordinand was admitted to the hermitage as a long-term resident,[239] the initiation master would call me over and say, "Jianyue, go and sit over there. Let this new arrival have your platform space."

I would obediently comply, picking up my robes and bowl, moving further back, and then seating myself once again. About a dozen more people entered the hall. Whenever a new person came in, I had to move further back. The final person to enter the Vinaya hall brought along a wooden double-sized bed that took up all of the remaining platform space, so I was ordered to move onto the floor and sit next to the verger, who was in charge of the incense and lanterns.[240]

I never uttered a single complaint, mentally treating the proceedings as a kind of game. When the other ordinands saw how meekly I was complying with the initiation master's orders, they criticized me for being such a spineless coward.

My response was: "The ability to endure humiliation is the foundation of spiritual cultivation. We are all undertaking the same precepts; hence, it is suitable that I make way for others."

Memorizing the Vinaya

The preparation period gradually drew to a close; the time when we were to be individually tested on our knowledge

---

239. Those who attend a monastic retreat are registered as long-term residents. Certain retreats like the yearly rains retreat (vassa) last for three months.

240. *xiangdeng*

Memorizing the Vinaya

of the Vinaya was approaching. We were expected to recite the entire text of *The Vinaya for Daily Use*. The novice initiation master placed me at the top of the recitation list, evidently expecting me to fail miserably and give up. All of my ordination brothers[241] were worried about me.

"You won't be able to recite the entire book, so why not ask the initiation master to move you to the last place?" they urged.

I replied, "Let's wait and see what happens tomorrow."

The next morning, the initiation master came in holding our name cards and led nine of us to the ordination preceptor.[242] First, I prostrated myself before him, after which, I recited the entire book in a ringing voice. The words flowed out effortlessly: it was just like tipping a bottle of water and letting the liquid pour forth freely without the least obstruction or hindrance.

The preceptor observed quizzically, "You have spent every day sitting silently, without uttering a word. You say that you are illiterate, yet you've just recited the entire book with absolute assurance and proficiency."

I explained my situation: "It isn't that I can't read—the real problem was lack of money to buy the textbook. I've been able to memorize the text by listening closely to the ordinand brothers seated next to me as they practised their recitation."

That pleased the preceptor enormously; as a reward, he offered me tea. When I went back to the study hall, all of the ordinands came over to congratulate me. There were thirteen class members with whom I got along especially well. All of them were able to recite the book with assurance.

---

241. Just as the precept and tonsure masters fulfill a parental role for novices, who are now bereft of their lay families, the members of a monastic's ordination class become their new siblings.

242. *jiaoshou shi*: This monastic assesses a novice's qualifications for ordination.

The Rambling Story of a Dream

Taking turns lecturing on the Brahmā's Net Sūtra[243]

During the retreat, a series of lectures was given on the *Brahmajāla-sūtra*.[244] Ācārya Xiangxue,[245] substituting for the abbot, sat facing the assembly. The four group heads (the head seat, the west hall, the rear hall, and the hall chief) took turns giving lectures.

One day, the head seat master, whose Dharma name was Leru, took the podium. His lecture was nothing more than a word-for-word reading of the Monk Sanmei's book, *Direct Exegesis*. He neither added nor omitted a single phrase, nor did he venture any explanation of the sūtra!

My ordinand comrades and I were sitting together in the same row. We exchanged amused glances with one another and couldn't suppress a few quiet chuckles. Observing our levity, Master Leru was deeply displeased. He strode back to the center of the hall and ordered the thirteen of us to take turns giving lectures.

Śrāmaṇera who have just undertaken the precepts are not normally expected to shoulder such a heavy responsibility. Clearly, Leru had issued this unprecedented command as a means of compelling us to come to him privately and humbly repent.

After the incident, three days passed, yet still no one came to beg his forgiveness. Our lack of response forced him to go ahead and submit a list of the offenders' names to the abbot. The Monk Sanmei construed the submission placed before him as high recommendation, so he benevo-

---

243. *Brahmajāla-sūtra*

244. The *Brahmajala Sūtra* enumerates ten major and forty-eight minor rules known as the bodhisattva precepts.

245. "Fragrant Snow"

lently permitted everyone on the list to give a lecture. Thus, it was a case of pretense turning into reality: once Sanmei's consent had been given, there was no turning back.

On the day that I was scheduled to lecture, every member of the inner and outer assembly was panic-stricken on my behalf. They all came to witness the debacle. The Monk Sanmei, Ācārya Xiangxue, and instruction master Xunliu were all seated in the back of the hall as compassionate onlookers.

I had been charged with lecturing on the contents of the tenth seat of faith from the first fascicle of the *Brahmā's Net Sūtra*. This passage concerns the ten seeds of the adamantine mental state. Opening the book, I began my lecture by reading the assigned text, after which I summarized the material and explained its virtue. Finally, I went through the passage and gave a word-by-word explanation. When I had finished, the audience below me called out their acclaim as a single voice. The Monk Sanmei and the other two masters were deeply pleased by my competent exegesis.

Afterwards, when I went to the abbot's room to extend my formal thanks, Sanmei presented me with bedding, clothing, and shoes.

Preceptor Xun wanted to know: "Under whose tutelage did you hear the sūtras?"

"When I was in Yun'nan," I replied, "I took dependance under my tonsure master, and then went on a pilgrimage to Baoqing prefecture, where I met Master Ziru. Ziru was giving a seminar on behalf of Grandmaster Zhuanyu, who had just written 'An Explanation of the Four Kinds of Reliance as Set Forth in the Śūraṅgama Sūtra.' I went along with him and listened to the lecture."

The Rambling Story of a Dream

Master Xun told me, "Grandmaster Zhuan was my ācārya when I was a novice monk, and Master Ziru is a close friend of mine. Why didn't you tell us earlier?!"

After that, Master Xun began taking me seriously. Right away, he gave Juexin robes and an alms-bowl as an alms donation and allowed him to enter the Vinaya study hall and receive the precepts.

Subduing demonic obstructions[246]

On the afternoon of the twentieth day of the third lunar month, a nephew from the Danyang county He clan came breezing into the hermitage. He was an arrogant young scholar who did not believe in the Three Jewels of Buddhism. He entered the hermitage in an inebriated state and burst into the abbot's quarters, whereupon he plunked himself down on the Monk's Dharma seat and laughed impudently. When an attendant came over and reprimanded him, he scolded the monk saucily. The temple monks were deeply offended by such disrespectful behavior and drove him out.

In retaliation, the scholar arranged to have a group of people come to the hermitage the next morning and cause a commotion. Due to this disruption, the retreat for the perfect precepts had to be summarily ended. Faced with imminent danger, Master Xun used expedient means[247] to peacefully resolve the situation and protect the monastery from ruin.

Normally, the late service at the temple was attended by lay people who wished to participate in Buddhist wor-

---

246. *Māra*-hindrances are any obstructions that prevent spiritual practitioners from realizing their Buddha nature.

247. *upāya* [Skt]: finding a teaching method suited to the mentality of one's listeners in order to inculcate the Buddha-Dharma

Subduing demonic obstructions

ship and acquire merit. Once the evening service was over, Master Xun called the participants together and led them to the sculpture of Skanda, the guardian bodhisattva who faces the statue of Buddha. Skanda is honored as a fierce Dharma protector.

Standing in front of the image, Master Xun told the group, "Today, our center for spiritual training has been thrown into a state of chaos by a demonic intrusion; under such circumstances, we cannot bring our goal of enlightenment to fruition. If any of you Buddhist disciples are willing to sacrifice your lives to safeguard the Dharma-gate, come forward now and help defend the monastery!"

Master Xun's entreaty was met with total silence. Elbowing aside the listeners, I stepped up to answer Master Xun's plea for help and prostrated myself before him.

Master Xun asked, "How can you possibly resolve this situation on your own?"

I ardently replied, "The countless disciples that the Monk has ordained are to be found everywhere under heaven. If one among us takes the initiative, all the rest of us will follow their example and jump into the fray.

"Monastics have left their homes: they have no wives to cherish, possess no property to be attached to, have no need to preserve personal fame or honor, nor do they treasure their own lives. They hold up their alms-bowls to fill their bellies and never need a cent for travel expenses; they can stay in monasteries rent-free.

"Ordained monks, holding the same precepts, are all part of the same family; the precepts are our common flesh and blood. Who among us wouldn't step up bravely to defend the Buddha's teachings! Whether it takes us a year or a decade, we're bound to get rid of that demonic gang eventually.

"You, Monk, and you two masters: rest assured that the situation is in good hands. There's no need for any temple administrators to worry about resolving the problem. We monks will handle it ourselves.

"If anyone in that demonic gang is willing to cast aside wife and property, and doesn't mind losing honor, fame, or even his own life—I invite him to come forward and see whether he can measure up to me. If not, both sides should work hard at their studies and nurture their respective moral foundations.

"Since ancient times, it has been known that by cultivating ethical behavior and literary prowess, any village scholar can achieve fame and honor and will enjoy greatness everywhere under heaven. Why would anyone want to sacrifice his own virtue over such a petty squabble?!"

Master Xun declared, "You've just taken on a weighty commitment in front of this group of people, and we'll expect you to keep your promise. Don't worry about lofty ideas like the purity of the Dharma-gate or eliminating demonic obstructions—just get the job done!!"

The monastic assembly dispersed. The lay people who had attended the evening service, having listened closely to our words, duly spread the message throughout the town.

The next day in the afternoon, over twenty townspeople turned up, all of whom were village elders or the heads of local academies. They had come to pay their respects to Preceptor Xun. I was asked to leave so that both sides could talk things over and reach an agreement.

The intended closing date for the retreat was not changed. As planned, it ended on the eighth day of the fourth lunar month.

After the retreat, the Monk convened a meeting in the abbot hall.

A gift for Sanmei

Addressing the two masters, as well as the highest-ranking senior monks who had been in his entourage for many years, he said, "If today's outbreak of demonic obstruction had not come to pass, Jianyue would not have come forward and demonstrated his ability. In order to protect the Buddha-Dharma and Dharma teachers, you, too, should evince the same courage and firmness of intention that he has shown. During this ordination retreat, I have found a person of true ability."

The group hearkened to his words, whereupon they formally thanked Sanmei and withdrew. The two masters pointed out our group of thirteen ordinands and indicated that henceforth, we would act as attendants to the Monk. They hoped that someday, we would all serve as staunch beams to support the Dharma-gate.

Painting a picture as a birthday gift for Sanmei

On the tenth day, we went back to the Yangzhou Shita Temple. The Huizhao Temple in Yangzhou had invited the Monk to preside over an ordination ceremony beginning on the twentieth day of the fourth lunar month.

The eighth day of the fifth lunar month was the monk Sanmei's grand birthday,[248] but neither I nor my thirteen ordinand comrades had any presents to give him.

I came up with an idea: "We can mount a scroll for him. I'll paint a portrait of Sudhana[249] on his pilgrimage to seek enlightenment. During his travels, he studied under fifty-

---

248. A "grand birthday" is celebrated every decade for those over the age of fifty.

249. The story of the Indian youth Sudhana is found in the Flower Garland Sūtra (*Buddhāvataṃsaka-nāma-mahāvaipulya-sūtra*).

three virtuous teachers. That will be our gift to the Monk. It will take me some time, so I won't be able to get to the Huizhao Temple with everyone to attend the beginning of the ordination."

Once the Monk Sanmei found out about our plan, he allowed me to use the abbot's chamber, where I could paint with a tranquil mind.

He remarked with a smile, "Jianyue, you've only just taken the precepts, but have already moved into my room!"

Shamefaced, I saluted Sanmei and thanked him.

On the twentieth day of the sixth lunar month, Lord Zheng of Haidao requested Sanmei's presence at the Shita Temple[250] to hold an Ullambana[251] assembly and lecture on the *Xiaoheng chao*[252] from the *Ullambana-sūtra*. Sanmei directed me to go to the Huizhao Temple as a replacement for the ācārya Xiangxue and instructed me to give a lecture on the *Direct Explanation of the Brahmajāla-sūtra*. Thus, Master Xiangxue would be free to return to the Shita Temple and substitute for the Monk by giving a lecture on the *Xiaoheng chao*. The retreats at the two temples both ended on the tenth day of the seventh lunar month.

---

250. Stone Pagoda Temple

251. The Ullambana festival is also called Saṃgha Day. It marks the ending of the summer retreat. An offering ceremony is held in which Buddhist laity present a meal to the Buddha and the saṃgha, thereby obtaining sufficient merit to liberate souls of the deceased from suffering.

252. *chao*: a summary of a larger text (in this case, a lengthy exposition on filial piety)

I keep my Dharma name

I do not change my Dharma name.

Master Xiang advised that new Dharma names[253] should be assigned to me and my fellow ordinands so that our affiliation would be evident when we served as Sanmei's attendants and carried out his work.[254] Accordingly, we went to the abbot's quarters as requested. My comrades all vied eagerly with one another to be the first to make obeisance to Sanmei and entreat him to bestow new Dharma names. I remained behind the others. Last of all, I prostrated myself at his feet.

Then, I knelt before the Monk and explained, "At my tonsure preceptor's behest, I formed the intention of leaving Yun'nan and travelling south in order to beg you, Monk, for the great precepts. If it hadn't been for this master, I would never have been tonsured and gone forth as a monk, nor would I have been qualified to receive full ordination and officially enter the saṃgha. I entreat you to show your great compassion and allow me to keep my old name so that I will never forget my origin. My intention is to dedicate my life to serving you as an attendant at your monastic seat."

The Monk[255] replied, "When I was first ordained, all of

---

253. Monks are given two double-character names by their tonsure master. The first dual-character name (*zihao*) is used by outsiders, whereas the Dharma name (*faming* or *fahui*) is used by senior monastics and masters when addressing the monk. Monks can also create names for themselves to show their personal spiritual intention.

254. Grandmaster Ouyi Zhixu (1599–1655) denounced this practice. Ven. Hongyi observes that Master Xiang demonstrated his rather vulgar mentality by insisting on new "trademark" names for Sanmei's attendants.

255. Throughout this narrative, Sanmei is referred to as the Monk (*heshang*), although he is sometimes designated by his style name in this translation. The appellation *heshang* originally signified an eminent monk qualified to assume the role of abbot, which seems to be the implication here. Sanmei's full name (i.e., *zihao* and *fahui*) was Sanmei Jiguang.

the monks who occupied the highest-ranking seats at the assembly urged me to request a new Dharma name from the Vinaya master. I considered the matter. My Vinaya master Ruxin[256] used the character *ru* ('thusness') in his Dharma name, I use the character *ji* ('silent', 'solitary'), while my tonsure preceptor uses the character *hai* ('ocean'). Like you, I did not want to forget my origin. The character *xing* ('suchness') would have taken generational precedence over the character *hai*,[257] so I decided to retain my old name.

"Since my ordination, I have spent over thirty years disseminating the Vinaya without meeting anyone who had similar scruples about changing their original monastic name. Today, I've finally encountered someone whose steadfast intention matches my own. This isn't self-deception! As a virtuous friend directing you on the path to enlightenment, my foremost consideration is putting moral principles into action. It makes no difference what your Dharma name is. You have my permission to keep your original name."

I am nominated to act as Preceptor Xun's replacement. My fellow Haichao ordinands' capable work generates an outstanding ordination. I learn the Vinaya by dint of bodhisattva insight.

At that time, the Vinaya hermitage of Taixing county requested an ordination retreat starting on the fifteenth day of the eighth lunar month. All of us newly-ordained monks went along as attendants.

---

256. Guxin Ruxin (1541–1615)

257. In the Baohua Mountain lineage gatha, 56 characters are assigned in succession to each succeeding generation of monastics. The character *xing* comes before the character *hai* on the list.

I replace Preceptor Xun

Prior to the event, Instructional Preceptor[258] Xun made a proclamation[259] to Sanmei on the evening of the tenth day, requesting that new officers[260] be assigned to supervise the groups of preceptees.[261]

He said, "I am currently teaching the novices,[262] but my health isn't up to it. I suffer from insufficiency of the middle *qi*;[263] my vital energy is gradually waning.

"You'll have to appoint someone else to teach and admonish the west hall group.[264] This trainer will oversee ordination affairs for every group of preceptees; his seat in the meditation hall will be with the first group of novices. Only Jianyue is qualified to fill such a position. Monk, please scrutinize and weigh the matter carefully."

The Monk immediately ordered his attendants to convene an assembly in the abbot's quarters. The participating monastics lined up in two columns[265] on the east and west sides of the abbot's seat. Sanmei then announced my appointment to the entire assembly.

---

258. *jiaoshou shi*

259. A saṃgha is a community that addresses temple affairs or carries out religious transactions in monastic gatherings known as karmans. Here, Preceptor Xun is making a formal proclamation to the saṃgha.

260. *zhishi*: The abbot's four main assistants respectively oversee four groups of monastics that are assigned to different parts of the meditation hall.

261. Preceptees were sorted into groups (*tang*), which were divided into two classes of nine preceptees each (*ban*).

262. He is the catechist (*jiaoshou*).

263. In traditional Chinese medicine, this condition is characterized by deficiency of the spleen and stomach energy. Some possible symptoms are lack of energy, poor appetite, coldness in the limbs, and weak vocal powers.

264. group: *tang*

265. For formal assemblies, monastics grouped themselves into eastern and western columns, with the south-facing abbot in the central position. On the abbot's left, the east column included the temple administrators. It faced the west column on the abbot's right, where the teaching monks were located. See *appendices*

The Rambling Story of a Dream

I knelt on the floor and stated my reservations: "I've only just received the full precepts this year on the eighth day of the fourth lunar month; not even six months have passed since then. How can I possibly shoulder such weighty responsibilities? How can someone with only a cursory understanding of the Vinaya and the Dharma serve as an instructor? Such an appointment would be harmful to the novices, and I'd be letting down the Monk who has shown me such bountiful compassion and kindness. Please choose someone else from among the senior monks to fill this post!"

The Monk replied, "I am well aware of your intention, conduct, and capacities, and approve of Preceptor Xun's recommendation. Even those who have arrived at the tenth *bhūmi*[266] still need to work for the well-being and spiritual growth of others. By spreading the Dharma, these adepts perfect their own consummate spiritual practice.

"So now, out of consideration for my own mission, why not continue your private studies while teaching others? Accepting this position will be beneficial in two ways: you will improve your own spiritual condition, while also improving the lives of others."

The two columns of monastics said in unison: "You should obey the Monk's compassionate order. You mustn't refuse again."

I had no choice but accept the commission.

Of my fellow ordinands, who had all been assigned the generation character 'ying,'[267] Cangwu served as the

---

266. The *Daśabhūmika Sūtra* enumerates ten levels of spiritual attainment for those on the path to Buddhahood. The *bhūmis* ('grounds') are progressive stages of cultivation.

267. see footnote 47.

I replace Preceptor Xun

retreat secretary; Huisheng, Yiren, Yuru, Ruoyu, Guanzhi, and the others acted as initiation masters.[268] Everyone got right to work, serious and dutiful. Among the Monk's many disciples, there had never been any as capable and enthusiastic as the group of comrades who had been ordained at the Haichao hermitage. Through their concerted effort, the retreat became a momentous event.

The senior monk Eryuan had been the initiation master at my ordination. Now, as the first group initiation instructor, his duty was to supervise ritual procedures. Although I was technically his superior, I still regarded him as my master and respectfully complied with his wishes in all things; for his part, he treated me with great humility. He left the final decisions regarding the meditation hall rules and procedures up to me and carried out my instructions.

But in my heart, I still felt shamefully inadequate. I hadn't the remotest idea of how to help enthusiastic students of the Vinaya to differentiate clearly between right and wrong. How could I guide them so that they gained confidence and contentment in their monastic vocation? One evening, preoccupied with these doubts, I went to Master Xun's quarters to pay him a formal visit.

After I had explained what was on my mind, the master told me, "In the Buddhist canon,[269] there are over a thousand Mahāyāna and Hīnayāna texts: I've never read them. Since your goal is to attain a thorough understanding of the Vinaya, you can request that books be sent to you so that you can study them. One day, you'll become a prominent Vinaya master. As the monk who identified you at the recent

---

268. *yinli*: the instruction masters who taught ordinands the correct protocol for every aspect of monastic life

269. *Tripiṭaka* [Skt]: "the three baskets"

The Rambling Story of a Dream

monastic assembly as the best candidate for this position, I am confident that you won't disappoint me."

Taking Master Xun's advice, I found someone to go to Jiaxing and procure a copy of *The Complete Vinaya* for me. From then on, I spent my days enforcing regulations in each group; by night, I would light a lantern, open a volume,[270] and study it exhaustively. When I encountered unfathomable passages in these ancient writings, it was agonizing not to have anyone to consult who was proficient in the exegesis of Buddhist texts. All that I could do was close the book and sigh. At such a time, my only recourse was to worship the bodhisattvas and pray that they would enlighten me. After laying my cares before the bodhisattvas, I would sit still for an instant, and then open the volume once again. Right away, clearly and beyond any doubt, the meaning would spring forth. It was like opening a door and beholding the mountains! Every time I ran into difficulties, this unfathomable insight would come to my aid.

I refuse a robe donated by my grateful class of novices.

The precept transmission assembly was scheduled to end on the fifteenth day of the eleventh lunar month. Three days before the close of the retreat, the novices from my group paid me a visit. Out of gratitude for my untiring instruction, they had made a yellow silk monastic robe as a present for me.[271]

---

270. Since woodblock printing reached a high point during the late Ming dynasty, the text in question was probably produced in this fashion. At that time, monastics at Jiaxing were working on woodblock prints for a new edition of the Buddhist canon.

271. Tailors lived and worked in larger monasteries. The novices probably hired someone to make their gift.

I refuse a donated robe

I told them, "The Monk and the catechist entrusted me with this weighty responsibility, so it was only correct that I should dedicate myself wholeheartedly to disseminating the Dharma-gate. I certainly did not act as a leader in order to attract fame or out of greed for special favors!"

I sternly refused to accept the robe. Still holding the article of clothing, they went to the abbot's quarters. Kneeling reverently, they explained to the Monk their reasons for presenting me with this gift.

Sanmei relayed their words to me: "The Vinaya prohibits attachments or actions done with the expectation of reward. There is no prohibition against giving alms voluntarily. You are allowed to accept this robe."

I explained, "I have refused to accept the robe for two reasons. First, I am ashamed that my practice of the precepts is so superficial, yet the responsibility laid upon me is so weighty. I fear that I have been inadequate in fulfilling the task entrusted to me and have failed in some respects. Those who perceive my shortcomings might make me a target for slander.

"Secondly, Monk, your Dharma-gate is lofty and stern. I fear that after this, anyone placed in charge of temple duties might take this as a precedent to justify accepting material rewards. In order to preclude that possibility, I will not receive the robe."

The Monk heard my argument with approbation and conveyed my words to the novices, saying, "The west hall master forbears to accept your gift in order to preserve his personal virtue and because he cherishes the Dharma-gate.[272] You mustn't insist that he accept your present!"

---

272. i.e., the Buddhist teachings

The Rambling Story of a Dream

On the eighteenth day, we went back to the Yangzhou Shita Temple with the Monk. The Chengtian Temple in Gaoyou[273] requested a precept transmission on the first day of the twelfth month. The retreat would last until the fifteenth day of the New Year. I continued to serve as the western hall master at that assembly.

---

273. a city in Yangzhou

Part Two

Master Xun requests that the Monk Sanmei bequeath the kāṣāya of Princess Rongchang to me.

On the seventeenth day of the first month, in the eleventh year of the Chongzhen regnal era,[274] we returned to Shita Temple. We received an invitation from the Shanqing hermitage, which was located in the same prefecture. They wanted us to hold an ordination retreat that would begin on the twentieth day of the first month and last until the middle of the third lunar month. Again, I was placed with the first group of novices. We also accepted an invitation from Baogong Temple in the town of Shaobo.[275] The retreat was to begin on the eighth day of the fourth month. I was assigned the duty of west hall master. When the assembly was over, we went back to the Shita Temple in Yangzhou.

Previously, during the seventh year of the Chongzhen regnal era, the Monk had been in Beijing disseminating the great precepts. Princess Rongchang,[276] the Wanli Emperor's daughter, and her husband, Prince Yang,[277] along with their entire retinue, came to take dependence[278] with Sanmei. They

---

274. 1638: Master Jianyue is now 37 years old.

275. in Yangzhou, now a city in Jiangsu province

276. Princess Rongchang (1582–1647) was the eldest child of the Ming dynasty Wanli Emperor.

277. Yang Chunyuan (1582–1616)

278. Taking dependence on a preceptor (*nissaya* [Skt]) means formally requesting to be apprenticed under a particular Buddhist mentor.

dispatched envoys to present three monastic robes[279] made of gold, paulownia, and purple fabrics to the abbot and the two ordination instructors. One robe was given to the Monk, one was for Ācārya Xiangxue, and one was for Preceptor Xunliu.

Now, Master Xun brought the robe that he had received from the princess and her husband to the abbot's room and made obeisance.

Tearfully, he declared, "I have served under you as a preceptor, Monk, for eleven years. During that time, I have paid close attention to those who have undertaken the precepts; I have observed their character and tested them in order to discern their mental state, actions, and conduct. My aim has always been to find a few candidates who qualify to assist you in promulgating your Dharma-gate.[280] Up until the present time, only one suitable monk has entered our order; he was ordained at the Haichao hermitage. It is Jianyue.

"As for myself, my appetite has been steadily decreasing and my life energy is dwindling. It is clear that I haven't long to live. I entreat you, Monk, to show compassion and allow me to bequeath to Jianyue the purple kāṣāya given to me by Princess Rongchang. If I can see with my own eyes someone taking my place, I will die content."

Sighing deeply, Sanmei told him, "You are truly my disciple, my right and left hand, whose great concern is ensuring the future of this Dharma-gate."

He immediately convened every official who had served in his entourage for many years to act as witnesses.

---

279. *sengjiali* (*saṃghāṭī* [Skt]): A heavy patchwork robe that could also be used as bedding. In this case, the robes would be inlaid with gold and worn by abbots for solemn rites.

280. Buddhist doctrine can be transmitted through many different teachings, or 'gates.'

Princess Rongchang's kāṣāya

The Monk then presented the robe to me with his own hands, saying, "You must serve me as faithfully as Preceptor Xun. If you do so, this Dharma-gate will prosper!"

Tears spilled down onto my collar as I prostrated myself and received the kāṣāya. The parents who gave me birth and master Xun, who recognized my worth and understood me—for me, the prodigious grace shown me by these people could only be repaid by promulgating the Dharma to benefit all sentient beings.

In the middle of the sixth lunar month, the Tandu Temple in the Qingjiangpu district of Huai'an[281] respectfully invited the Monk to come and lead an ordination. That assembly ended on the nineteenth day of the seventh month, at which time Sanmei wished to visit the Donghai Yuntai Temple on Yuntai Mountain. He ordered me to stay behind at the Tandu Temple, where I would supervise the completion of ordination licenses, compile and distribute the ordination yearbook,[282] and then dismiss the assembly. Once these tasks had been accomplished, I followed Sanmei to Yuntai Mountain. In the eighth lunar month, I rejoined the Monk and gave him a report on the completion of these projects. On the thirteenth day, we descended the mountain, crossed the sea, and returned to Shita Temple.

---

281. in Jiangsu province

282. *tongjie lu*: Holmes Welch calls this ordination record a 'yearbook.' Containing the names and some personal details about the presiding officers and preceptees who attended an ordination, these documents were treasured by their recipients.

Holmes Welch, *The Practice of Chinese Buddhism,* 1900–1950 (Cambridge: Harvard University Press, 1973) 250–251. https://terebess.hu/zen/mesterek/Holmes-Welch-The-Practice.pdf

The Rambling Story of a Dream

Holding an ordination at the Bao'en Temple in Nanjing

There were several magistrates in Nanjing who were Dharma-protectors. They invited us to hold an ordination at the Bao'en Temple starting on the fifteenth day of the tenth month. Master Xunliu had to remain at Shita Temple due to poor health. I took care of him and served him herbal decoctions.

For this precept transmission assembly, the Monk entered Nanjing accompanied by Master Duxing serving as the ācārya and Master Xiangxue, who acted as the preceptor. They sent a messenger back to Shita requesting that I go to the ordination, but I refused adamantly and stayed where I was. Later on, they again sent word that I was needed at the ordination.

Master Xun, whose temperament was exceedingly filial, told me, "Although I am seriously ill, you mustn't go against the Monk's compassionate orders. I would like to entrust you with one commission: after my death and cremation, see that my remains are sent to the Tianlong Temple in Nanjing and buried on the right side of the Vinaya Patriarch's stūpa."[283]

Hearing his words, tears of sorrow rolled unchecked down my cheeks. I didn't want to leave him.

Again, Master Xun told me, "This is the Monk's first trip to Nanjing, so there must be a crowd of people requesting the precepts. This message is the second urgent request for your help; clearly, you will be entrusted with weighty responsibilities. Don't delay any longer—you must depart right away."

Thus, I had to take leave of Master Xun and go to Nanjing.

---

283. The Vinaya patriarch, Guxin Ruxin, is interred in a stūpa at the Tianlong Temple.

Managing the novice quarters

I assign spaces to ordinands and exhort them to maintain proper comportment.

When the Monk asked me about Master Xun's condition, I reported that he was gravely ill. Once again, I was appointed to serve as the west hall teacher.[284] Additionally, Master Xiangxue assigned me the duty of instructing and managing the novices. Over six hundred people who had never received the preliminary precepts were attending the ordination. The novice quarters were located on the western side of the compound behind the Three Saints Hall.[285]

The Monk told me, "So many people have come that the two ācāryas couldn't assign each one a place[286] and get them seated in rows. Go down there now and get everything organized."

I immediately went as requested and found that luggage had been dumped higgledy-piggledy all over the meditation hall. Most of the participants had previously attended Dharma lectures, but not one among them had ever cultivated proper monastic decorum. They were used to behaving[287] in an unruly, arrogant manner.

I had to avoid ruffling any feathers so that they would heed my instructions; hence, I approached them in a cautiously self-effacing manner.

Addressing the crowd of preceptees, I told them: "I have been sent here by the Monk. It is with great reluctance that

---

284. the senior monk in charge of the group of ordinands seated on the west platform of the meditation hall

285. The "saints" were probably three buddha images.

286. Each participant was assigned a *tatami*-sized space for their mat.

287. Buddhist psychology posits ingrained tendencies that have been formed over many lifetimes due to an accretion of habitual actions and thoughts. The goal of spiritual practice is to eradicate this karmic residue.

I serve as the west hall leader. So now, I'd like to talk things over with all of you so that we can work together.

"You must be willing to follow the rules and live together harmoniously; if not, there will be no way for me to train you. Please take a good look at this hall. The middle area is broad and spacious; it must be kept clear so that hundreds of people can come and go freely. With a central thoroughfare kept open, the platform space allotted to each participant will inevitably be extremely cramped. There won't be enough space for so many people to lie down and sleep. If most of you expect to sleep on pallet beds, what will everyone else do?

"I think that our best option is to begin by assigning places on the floor. Those among you who harbor a sincere intention to receive the precepts should willingly make way for others. By doing so, you will manifest selflessness and put your bodhisattva vows into practice. Now, please follow the numbered spaces that I'll assign and take your places on the floor. You should organize yourselves into straight horizontal rows; make sure that the space between the rows is kept even.

"If you are from the capital city or have brought a small bed, come here tomorrow and occupy the places that will be assigned to you today. Those who have come from outside the capital or don't have small beds can use a meditation platform. I hope that everyone will behave quietly and peacefully. No disorderly conduct is allowed!!"

Everybody followed my instructions with good cheer. No one jostled anyone else or scrambled to get settled. Over six hundred people were staying in that large hall. They kept to their assigned places and maintained straight, orderly rows. The hall layout looked like a system of neatly arranged

I act as an ordination witness

streets and alleyways. You could see a vista laid out clearly from one end of the hall to the other! Every night when I gave explanatory lectures on the Vinaya, and whenever I taught or admonished them during the daytime hours, the entire group took in my instruction with deference.

I act as one of the witnessing ācāryas at the ordination ceremony.

When the ordinands found out that seven witnesses[288] would be present at their ordination ceremony, the śrāmaṇera[289] who functioned as their class head held a conference with the group. This monk's name was Xiaoyuan. He was fifty years of age and came from Jingzhou prefecture. In Nanjing, he had been attending Dharma lectures and sūtra readings for quite some time. He wanted me to act as one of the reverend witnesses at the coming ordination. This proposal met with everyone's approval, so the entire group went to see the abbot.

They knelt before the Monk and made their request. Sanmei accordingly sent one of his attendants to me to convey the group's proposal.

I declared, "As your disciple, only two summers[290] have passed since my ordination, not to mention that my spiritual practice is superficial, and I have yet to accumulate any meritorious fruits of virtuous action. I wouldn't dare to stand among the reverend witnesses."

Sanmei overruled my reservations: "It is the sincere wish of hundreds of ordinands. Accepting the position does

---

288. Three preceptors and seven witnesses must be present on the ordination platform.
289. a novice who has undertaken ten preliminary precepts
290. i.e., having attended only two summer *varṣa* retreats

not imply any presumption on your part—you would not be usurping anyone's place. So, there's no need for you to refuse their request. Karmic circumstances have given rise to this appointment!"

I had no choice but to bow and thank him.

Harsh disciplinary measures are taken against delinquent monks. The ordination ceremony tallies perfectly with the dream that I had when I first went forth as a renunciate.

At the Three Saints Shrine, which was in the west hall nearby the temple business office and kitchen, porridge was served three times a day. The preceptees took their meals in order according to their assigned places in the meditation hall.

One day at the 7 AM mealtime hour, the monk assigned to refectory duty never brought our food. I looked into the matter and discovered that the meal server had tried to exact payment from the novices for their meals. When his demands were not met, he deliberately caused mischief. I got hold of him immediately and punished him by making him kneel with his hands folded at his chest for the length of time measured by burning an incense stick.

Over a hundred people worked in the kitchen. When they found out what had befallen their co-worker, they banded together and left the western hall *en masse*.

At that, I went straight to Master Qixuan. He was from the Central Buddhist Registry[291] and acted as the monastic discipline supervisor. When I reported the situation, he immediately ordered the temple administrators to have

---

291. *senglusi*

Escorting Master Xun's relics to Tianlong Temple

every gate closed. Then, he had the head cook and the rice steward locked into wooden cangues. Meanwhile, some of the fleeing offenders were apprehended and locked up, while others evaded capture by scrambling over the temple wall and dashing off.

Back in those days in the capital city, heavy punitive measures were commonly exacted during retreats in every monastery kitchen and hall.

Once the miscreants had been chastised, discipline and sobriety ensued. The kitchen staff now followed the regulations scrupulously. No one dared to cause any further trouble.

On the day of the formal ordination ceremony, everything that happened accorded exactly with the events that I had seen in my dream on that momentous night when I had just gone forth from secular life.

We escort Master Xun's remains to their final resting place.

While the Vinaya transmission was in progress, news suddenly reached us that Master Xun had already entered *nirvāṇa*[292] at the Shita Temple. His remains were now being transported to the Tianlong Temple; the funeral escort had already reached the Nanmen Bridge.

Remembering my benefactor's kindness, I was heartbroken and cried uncontrollably. I immediately went to intercept the funeral party with my thirteen ordinand comrades. When we caught up with the funeral cortège, we took Master Xun's remains to the Pude Temple for temporary safekeeping. Master Daosheng stayed at the temple to

---

292. the state in which all illusions and karma have been extinguished

keep vigil over the coffin and burn incense. These matters settled, my comrades and I went back to the Bao'en pagoda.

At the foot of the Porcelain Tower pagoda, altars were set up in the eight directions. One hundred monks surrounded the altars and performed continuous repentance rites for a week.

On the first day of the twelfth month, a procession took place in which a throng of novices was led by the Monk, two ācāryas, the high-ranking monks, and me and my ordination brothers. Hanging banners marked the head of the procession, and each participant carried incense and flowers. Over a thousand people were in attendance. As the funeral cortège bore the Master's relics to Tianlong Temple, the voice of the Buddha was heard continuously. Thus, in fulfillment of Master Xun's last directive, his relics were transported to the Tianlong Temple.

When the precept transmission concluded, Duke Fan, the minister of war, respectfully invited Sanmei to stay at the Yihua hermitage. The duke chose New Year's Day as an auspicious date on which to hold ceremonies for taking refuge[293] and receiving the five minimal precepts for the laity. Along with the rest of the party, I took leave of the Monk and returned to the Shita Temple.

Baohua Monastery[294]

On the ninth day of the new year,[295] the Monk undertook the return trip to Shita Temple by boat. The voyagers met with gale winds at Longtan and had to halt midway for three days.

---

293. a ceremony in which one formally takes refuge in the Buddha, the Dharma and the Sangha

294. daochang (bodhi-maṇḍa [Skt]): Buddhist monastery

295. 1639, in Jianyue's 38th year

Baohua Monastery

During their three-day stopover, a monk from the Ding'shui hermitage by the name of Chuxi came to pay his respects. He was the Dharma-grandson of Grandmaster Miaofeng. The Shenzong Emperor[296] had ordered Grandmaster Miaofeng to oversee the construction of a bronze hall on Baohua Mountain. Chuxi had come to convey an invitation to the Monk, respectfully asking him to come and visit Mount Baohua.[297]

The Monk agreed to accompany him to the monastery, only to discover that the roads were covered in weeds and the stairs and hall foundations were damaged. Few lanterns and incense burners were lit in the main temple hall, and the hallways were empty and silent. Scarcely any people were to be seen; everything was pervaded by an air of desolation and ruin.

Sighing, the Monk exclaimed, "This monastery was built less than fifty years ago,[298] yet it's already in such a miserable state!"

Chuxi replied, "There has been a dearth of virtuous people to serve as temple officials. I implore you, Monk, in your great benevolence and compassion, to revive this foundering monastery. The spirit of our departed patriarch will be deeply grateful for your intercession."

The Monk generously gave his consent, and then headed back down the mountain. The next day, he crossed the river and returned to the Shita Temple in Yangzhou.

---

296. the Wanli Emperor (r. 1572–1620)

297. *suixi*: Temple visits were carefully noted on a monastic's ordination certificate or ordination yearbook. By visiting temples, one acquired merit.

298. The bronze hall was commissioned in 1605 by the Empress Dowager Xiaoding, mother of the Wanli Emperor.

The Rambling Story of a Dream

Sanmei is formally requested to stay at Baohua as a permanent resident.

The Jiangyin county Shifang hermitage conveyed a respectful invitation to Sanmei, requesting him to lead a Dharma transmission starting on the eighth day of the second month. Master Xiangxue would act as the karman master,[299] overseeing the formal profession of the precepts, and I served as the instructional preceptor for the first time.

It wasn't until 1639 that I officially became an instruction master.[300] My responsibilities were announced by the Monk in the presence of the entire corps of monastery officials.

"From now on," he proclaimed, "anyone who intends to undertake the precepts and wants to be registered for platform space in the ordination training hall[301] must apply directly to you; furthermore, all decisions regarding candidates for administrative[302] posts in any of the outer monastery halls will also be the exclusive responsibility of the instruction master. You don't have to report back to me on these proceedings."

Clearly, these were weighty tasks, and I would be expected to handle many different monastery affairs. I construed the Monk's sudden announcement as arising from compassion. I was also determined not to let Master Xunliu down, since he had recognized my ability and recommended me. Thus, I accepted these responsibilities on behalf of both masters.

---

299. *jiemo shi*

300. *jiaoshou shi*

301. *bantang*: These responsibilities are not clearly elucidated in the text. The precentor (*weina*) managed the meditation hall and appointed minor officials, which might be viewed as an analogous case. *see* appendices

302. *zhishi*

Sanmei becomes a permanent resident of Baohua

In the middle of the second month, Chuxi and several other people from Mount Baohua[303] brought letters to the Shifang hermitage from every Dharma protector and lay Buddhist in Nanjing. They petitioned the Monk to come to Mount Baohua as a permanent resident. Since the Monk had already acceded to the request, he did not make any more refusals.

Once that had been settled, the Monk ordered the guest prefect[304] to take Chuxi and his contingent on a tour of the temple's residence halls. When they got to my quarters, everyone in the group gave me an intense stare.

Perceiving their reaction, I told them, "During the winter of the seventh Chongzhen regnal year,[305] I was studying a sūtra on your mountain. Sorry for disturbing all of you permanent residents!"

Laughing, they replied, "When we first saw you, your face seemed rather familiar, but we feared that we might be mistaken. So, it's you, after all! How did you manage to get promoted to such a high position so quickly? We have eyes, yet we blindly failed to see your ability!"

After that, the conversation turned to a discussion of the events that had transpired at Baohua during the years since my leave-taking. The next day, the group went back to the mountain. The ordination retreat at the Shifang hermitage concluded on the eighth day of the fourth month.

---

303. As the only temple in the Baohua hills, Baohua monastery was referred to as the "mountain."

304. *zhibin shi*

305. 1634, when Jianyue was 33 years of age

The Rambling Story of a Dream

The Monk Sanmei takes over the command of Baohua Mountain. I am requested to act as the instruction master, as well as the prior,[306] but I stipulate that four conditions be met before I accept the two positions.

On the fifteenth day, the Monk arrived at Baohua Mountain. That evening, he convened a group consisting of Master Jianxuan, Master Zhifu, Master Sihong, Master Chunran, Master Duxing, Master Xinrong, Master Xiangxue, Master Yuegu, Master Dazhao, along with several elderly ācāryas and me. Together, we went to the abbot's quarters[307] for a discussion.

Addressing the group, the Monk declared, "We are now installed on this mountain as permanent residents. Our present status is entirely different from the position as temporary residents that we previously held at the Shita Temple. Among you all, I will now appoint a candidate whose intention is firmly set upon enlightenment. This monk, the superintendent,[308] will oversee the temple's internal and external affairs. I need someone of exceptional ability who is robustly energetic and will spare no effort to keep the entire monastery running smoothly.

"As for the rest of you officials in the east and west ranks, your duties will be decided in due course. That's all for the moment."

Upon hearing this announcement, everyone just stood mutely in their places.

Then, the Monk addressed me directly: "Jianyue, why haven't you volunteered to undertake this responsibility?"

---

306. *jianyuan*: temple superintendent
307. The temple hall where the abbot held meetings was known as the abbot's room.
308. *jianyuan*

I assume weighty responsibilities at Baohua

I replied, "Monk, you never called my name, and I didn't dare to put myself forward in front of these eminent masters."

At this, the Monk returned, "I specified quite clearly that the positions would require firm Way-intention, exceptional ability, and unstinting effort. Who else could possibly measure up to such requirements!"

All of the ācāryas affirmed, "Master Jian, you'd better bow and accept the appointment with thanks. You cannot refuse the Monk's compassionate order again!"

I happily complied with the master's order.

Bowing to the Monk, I declared, "Your disciple Jianyue only dares to take on this responsibility under four conditions: First, I will uniformly take my three meals of congee with the saṃgha and never keep visiting almsgivers company at meals; secondly, I will never receive or see off visiting dignitaries; third, I will never attend the funerals or weddings of laypeople; and fourth, I will not personally handle any money that is received or paid out by the temple for purchases or other transactions.

"With the exception of these four limitations, I will devote myself wholeheartedly to managing the affairs of the saṃgha. I will never be neglectful of any matter that concerns the community of resident monks."

The Monk responded, "The four conditions that you have set will be met accordingly, but you cannot decline the role of Vinaya teaching master."

I countered, "My duties have never included the supervision of Vinaya instruction. I fear that due to my lack of experience, the saṃgha will be dissatisfied with your decision."

The Monk replied, "As of now, you are the instruction master, as well as the prior. Those offices have nothing to do with the supervision of instructors."

The Rambling Story of a Dream

The group of ācāryas declared, "Presently, the one among us teaching the Vinaya is none other than you, which is all the more reason to accept the Monk's compassionate assignment."

Chengzhuo comes to the mountain to receive the precepts.

On the eighteenth day of the fifth lunar month, the Monk's sixtieth grand birthday was celebrated. For the great occasion, high-ranking monastics from temples and hermitages came from far and wide, and Buddhist disciples from the ten directions gathered at Mount Baohua.

The winter term of the Buddhist calendar started on the ninth month.

Unexpectedly, Chengzhuo arrived on the mountain carrying his robes and bowl. I was overjoyed at his sudden arrival and wanted to know where he'd been.

He filled me in on his recent activities: "After we became separated during the northern insurrections, I journeyed south alone to the Tiantong Temple for meditation training. Afterwards, I went back to Mount Huang to study the scriptures, biding my time until it was safe to travel.

"I've come here directly from the Huang mountains.[309] All along the route, I've been inquiring about your whereabouts, but was never able to locate you."

I explained, "You couldn't find me because I've changed my name to Jianyue.

"So, we were together, then we got separated, and now we're together once again. This miraculous reunion can

---

309. the Yellow Mountains

only have come about due to multiple lifetimes of auspicious causation! By losing touch with me for three years, you've given me enough time to qualify as one of the seven reverend witnesses at your ordination!"

Great authority utilizes expedient means to bring me back to Baohua.

The Jiangnan area was in a state of severe drought during the thirteenth year of the Chongzhen regnal era.[310] The spring term closed on the eighth day of the fourth month.

Duke Su, a high-ranking palace eunuch from the inner court, and others came to Mount Baohua. As an alms donation, they provided the temple monks with a vegetarian banquet. The temple's resident monks used the donation to purchase coarse, discolored flour. The Monk commanded that I be brought to his quarters, whereupon he summarily berated me for negligence.

He was just lifting a hand to strike me when I protested: "Monk, have you forgotten your humble disciple's requests that you yourself granted before I assumed my present responsibilities?"

The Monk gave the point some thought and finally conceded, "This mess has nothing to do with you!"

He then went straight to the deputy superintendent's quarters and gave Master Dazhao a good thrashing. Afterwards, Master Da came to my dormitory in a towering rage, blaming me for not covering up his error. As it happened, I was indebted to Master Da for acting as one of the reverend witnesses at my ordination.

---

310. 1640, when Jianyue was 39 years old

The Rambling Story of a Dream

I explained the awkward situation to Chengzhuo: "Right now, the only way to circumvent this difficulty is to get out of here. We'd better go to Tiantong Temple."

Before sunrise the next day, I entrusted my luggage to Chengzhuo, who would descend via the back side of the mountain and wait for me.

At dawn, I ascended Dragon Hill and made nine prostrations in the direction of the abbot's quarters; then, I went down the mountain and rejoined Chengzhuo. We proceeded to the Tangshui Yanxiang Temple, where we stayed the night. After four days of travel, we arrived at Wuxi county and lodged at the Zhentang hermitage. A few of the disciples there urged us to stay longer and rest for a while.

On the twentieth day of the fourth month, a newly-ordained disciple from Mount Baohua came to the hermitage. Upon seeing me, he prostrated himself tearfully. We asked him why he had come.

His explanation was: "When you monks left on the ninth day, the Monk told the saṃgha that you oughtn't to have made off with that sum of forty silver *liang* that had been provided for the great assembly. There was much discussion and debate amongst the Baohua temple residents. I couldn't refrain from asserting that you'd been wrongfully accused of misconduct—that's why I'm crying."

To the visitor and Chengzhuo, I declared, "The Monk isn't really blaming me. Out of great compassion, the old fellow is using expedient means[311] to make me return to the temple without being summoned. If I don't go back, the monks will assume that the rumor is true."

---

311. *upāya* [Skt.]

The pennant of Buddhism is erected

The next day, I went back to Mount Baohua and prostrated myself at the abbot's feet, humbly entreating his forgiveness. The Monk replied, "You haven't done anything wrong, so there's nothing to forgive. You had no choice but to leave. I only said that you'd made off with the silver to spur you into action. My stratagem worked really quickly!"

At that, the Monk had me assume my previous instructor duties once again.

The pennant of Buddhism is erected on Mount Baohua.

When the winter term began, a group of over a hundred novices received the bhikṣu precepts;[312] right afterwards, four aspirants from the north also came to undertake the precepts. The Monk ordered Master Xiangxue, the ācārya, to confer the ten śrāmaṇera precepts.[313] After complying with the monk's request, Xiang Ācārya went ahead and conferred the bhikṣu precepts, as well. Zhixian, the induction master,[314] brought these ordinands to my quarters, made obeisance, and then reported on the ordination.

I told him, "The Vinaya sets forth clear rules regarding ordination procedures. While the Monk is still alive, how can you possibly take matters into your own hands and confer the final precepts on four ordinands with only one master in attendance!? I'm not your catechist, and I cannot issue ordination certificates or ordination yearbooks for this group."

---

312. *bhikṣu-saṃvara* [Skt.] 250 rules of moral conduct undertaken by male monks.

313. *śrāmaṇera-saṃvara* [Skt.]

314. *yinli shi*: one of the assistant ordination instructors who teaches novices the proper demeanor and the required procedures for every aspect of daily life in the monastery

The Rambling Story of a Dream

Hearing this, Zhixian went back to Master Xiang and told him my response. Xiang Ācārya then upbraided me vehemently for arrogance and dereliction of duty to my superiors. He went straight to the Monk to report on the situation. The Monk promptly sent an attendant to summon me, and then interrogated me on why I had refused to cooperate.

I declared, "The scolding that your humble disciple got from Master Xiang arose because he is judging me by secular standards. I, Jianyue, adhere strictly to Buddhist regulations. It is a grave lapse for one instructor to take matters into his own hands and confer the full precepts without having ten masters present on the ordination platform. The flourishing and decay of the Dharma-gate is at stake here."

"As a catechist," I concluded, "I, your lowly servant, am duty bound to halt such erroneous proceedings and admonish the parties involved. Monk, please weigh this matter carefully!"

The Monk turned to Master Xiang, saying, "Enough! The fault lies with you; Jianyue's judgement is absolutely correct. You'll have to find another time to confer the full precepts when the required ten masters can be present on the ordination platform!"

Afterwards, he addressed the monastery officials and those who occupied the highest-ranking seats in assemblies: "With Jianyue to give his clear judgements, this old monk can finally establish the pennant of Buddhism on Mount Baohua!"

Repositioning the temple by the labor of my own hands

In the fourteenth year of the Chongzhen regnal era,[315] the Chaoguo Temple located in Songjiang prefecture reverently

---

315. 1641: Jianyue was 40 years old.

invited the Monk to lead an ordination retreat that would begin on the fifteenth day of the first month. An assembly of over five hundred new and longstanding followers would be present. Additionally, the Guangfu Temple of Fushan, located in Changshu county, contacted the Monk during the retreat and requested an ordination at their temple. They had selected the twenty-eighth day of the fifth month for the event.

The retreat at Songjiang ended on the fifteenth day of the fifth month, at which time the Monk ordered me to lead the ordination officials to the Guangfu Temple in advance of the rest of the party. That retreat ended on the first day of the seventh month. At the close of the retreat, we went back to Mount Baohua.

Baohua Temple had been commissioned by imperial decree. The entire construction process had been carried out under the supervision of eunuchs from the inner court, who had positioned the temple in an inharmonious direction. Due to their faulty planning, the temple had never flourished; there was a chronic paucity of resident monastics.

In order to correct this defect, the Monk selected an auspicious day for reorienting the temple. Every architectural feature was to be realigned, with the exception of the bronze hall,[316] which was left in its original location. In terms of cost, labor, and engineering, it was a prodigious undertaking.

While the project was underway, the Guanyin hermitage on Xixia Mountain, where the Vinaya Patriarch Guxin had been tonsured, sent a respectful invitation to the Monk, requesting him to conduct a retreat for them beginning on the eighth day of the twelfth lunar month. Although

---

316. commissioned by the Ming-dynasty dowager empress Xiaoding (1545–1614)

The Rambling Story of a Dream

I was serving as the catechist at this assembly, the Monk would still send me back to Mount Baohua from time to time. Tiles had to be removed and transported to the new location; every last part of the building had to be manually dismantled and relocated. I personally took the lead in carrying out the hard labor.

I flee Mount Baohua.

The retreat at Xixia ended on the tenth day of the new year,[317] whereupon we returned to Mount Baohua.

A disciple of the guest master Lüzhong was the verger who was in charge of incense and lanterns in the front hall. This disciple's actions were not in keeping with the Vinaya. Xiang Ācārya, Master Dazhao, the business office manager,[318] and I discussed the monk's lapses and considered how to deal with the situation. Both masters concurred in deciding to overlook the monk's misbehavior.

When I heard their judgement, I was bitterly disappointed. The monk had violated the fundamental precepts, yet his superiors were going to pardon him. Allowing such transgressions to pass without any consequences heralded the annihilation of the Vinaya and the Buddha-Dharma. My only recourse was to retreat to Mount Huang to preserve the integrity of my own spiritual practice.

I immediately explained the situation to Chengzhuo, who advised, "Don't be too hasty about adopting a course of action."

I replied, "I am deeply indebted to the benevolent Baohua monks and am loathe to part from them. At present, all of

---

317. 1642: Jianyue was now 41 years old.
318. *dangjia*

I flee Mount Baohua

the Monk's high-ranking staff—the ācāryas, the group leaders, and the business office manager—are my teachers and elders. I'm only a disciple; moreover, I'm from Yun'nan. It's best to get out of here as quickly as possible."

Having made my decision, I went to the abbot and announced that I was taking a leave of absence and would be departing from Mount Baohua in order to do an intensive retreat. The Monk did not give his permission; rather, he bid me accompany him to Qizhou[319] in the Chu region. The King of Jing[320] had extended a courteous invitation to the Monk, requesting him to come and hold an ordination.

I told the Monk, "Today, I have given preliminary notice of my absence. My departure time has yet to be set."

Whatever happened, my mind was made up: I couldn't stay there. I absolutely had to leave. The next morning, four of us—Chengzhuo, Tianyi, Changqing, and I—packed up our robes and alms-bowls and set off together for Mount Huang. We got to the Wuli Pagoda tea hermitage in Taiping county, where we encountered Xiangliu, a disciple of Gengshi.

As it happened, Qingyun cliff, on which Master Chongde resided, was right across from us. Next to this mountain was a hill that was densely covered in emerald pine woods. Surrounded by mountains, it was serene and secluded. The disciple invited us to stay and conduct our spiritual practice in this tranquil location. Accordingly, Chengzhuo and I cut wild thatching grasses, cleared the ground for a foundation, and built ourselves a tiny dipper-shaped hut. It took us a month to complete the work.

---

319. Qi prefecture: in modern Hubei

320. a feudal title conferred upon Chu Ciyan. The tenth-generation title-holder, he died in 1642.

The Rambling Story of a Dream

But once we'd finished building our hut, it suddenly occurred to me that we had set off with the firm resolution of going to Mount Huang. Why had we stopped along the way like this?! Seeing that I had changed my mind, Tianyi decided to return to Mount Baohua. Chengzhuo had been invited to Jingde county, so we, too, parted ways. Only Changqing stayed with me, coming along as my attendant.

On the tenth day of the tenth month, Gengshi escorted us to Mount Huang. We took up residence at the Beiye hermitage[321] of the Mañjuśrī monastery. Mount Huang[322] is extremely rocky and has very little soil; hence, nary a stalk of vegetables would grow, and there wasn't the slightest chance of getting any fresh produce to eat. By the twelfth lunar month, as far as the eye could see, there was nothing but an endless expanse of silver peaks and jade ridges. Mount Huang's winter temperatures are as frigid as those of the northern regions beyond the Great Wall.

Xiaozong, the meditation master at the Mañjuśrī monastery, was a disciple of the ordination preceptor. He found out that during the wintertime on Mount Baohua, I never stayed close to a stove to warm myself. Concerned about my well-being, he made a special trip to our retreat site, treading through snow with bags of rice and charcoal on his back. When he arrived, he knelt on the floor and begged me to warm myself next to a stove. So earnest was his entreaty that I agreed to follow his advice.

Although it was bitterly cold there, it was an eminently suitable location for spiritual cultivation. That is why I never for a moment considered leaving the mountain.

---

321. perhaps named after the Sanskrit plant *pattra*, upon which early Buddhist texts were recorded

322. Yellow Mountain

Back to Baohua

It was the beginning of spring in the sixteenth Chongzhen regnal year.[323] On the eleventh day of the first lunar month, Gengshi brought a party coming from Mount Baohua to the Beiye hermitage where I was staying. The group consisted of Master Jiesheng, a meditation supervisor with whom I had formed a close bond, along with his two disciples, Zhi and Zhou.

As soon as I caught sight of the visitors, I exclaimed, "What on earth has brought you here?!"

Master Jie rejoined, "Master Preceptor,[324] after you left Baohua, the Monk spent twenty-six days in Qizhou, in the Chu region. In the new year, he returned to Mount Baohua on the second day of this month. Upon learning that this humble servant was on excellent terms with you, Master Preceptor, he wrote a letter with his own hand, requesting that I deliver it to you directly and escort you back to Mount Baohua."

I immediately lit some incense and received the letter with both hands upraised. With utmost solemnity, I read the Monk's letter. Like a compassionate father who never abandons his wayward son, he had written me a letter brimming with gracious kindness. I was profoundly moved.

For five days, I kept Master Jiesheng company as my guest and took him on mountain tours. Then, we travelled to Jingde county together to meet Chengzhuo. We stayed with Chengzhuo for over a month, enjoying that peaceful sanctuary and picking tea leaves. On the seventh day of the third month, we finally returned to Mount Baohua.

---

323. 1643, when Jianyue was 42 years old
324. *jiaoshou shi*: preceptor, catechist

The Rambling Story of a Dream

The Monk had received an invitation from Xingjiao Temple in Yangzhou prefecture and had already crossed the river to start an ordination assembly.

Before his departure, he left these instructions: "When Jianyue gets back, have him go to the ordination and serve as the novice preceptor."

Since the retreat had begun on the first day of the third month and the rector[325] Xuan had already taken over the responsibility, my help was no longer required, so I stayed at Mount Baohua and awaited the Monk's return. In the meantime, I sent the disciples Zhi and Zhou across the river[326] to pay their respects to the Monk in acknowledgement of his previous orders. They were to extend my salutations.

When it was nearly time for the retreat masters to mount the ordination platform and confer the bhikṣu precepts, I received another gracious summons from the Monk requesting my presence there. When I arrived, I repented for the violation of disobeying the master's orders. The Monk took pity on me and happily forgave my offense. He then made me mount the ordination platform to act as one of the reverend witnesses.

I substitute for the Monk at the Guanyin hermitage.

After the Yangzhou ordination retreat had come to a close, the Kou'anda Temple in Taizhou[327] invited the Monk to come and transmit the precepts. As before, I served as the catechist. The Maqiao Guanyin hermitage was not far from

---

325. *shangzuo*
326. Mount Baohua lies on the southern bank of the Yangtze River.
327. located in modern Zhejiang province

Kou'an Great Temple.[328] That temple, too, invited the Monk to hold a precept transmission; he accepted their invitation. Once the Kou'an Temple retreat was accomplished, we went to the hermitage.

One day, the Monk was invited to the home of a local bureaucrat named Zhu. At that time, many were coming to take reliance and request Buddhist names, so before his departure, the Monk left me his own robe and a pre-selected list of Dharma names. When supplicants arrived, I was to don the master's robe, sit in his Dharma seat, and assign a Buddhist name from the list to each supplicant. As it happened, the weather was overcast and rainy for two days straight. Not a single person came to the hermitage, so I never had to sit upon the Monk's seat of authority, nor did I assign any Dharma names.

As soon as the Monk returned, the sun came out and there was a continuous stream of people coming to take reliance and obtain Buddhist names.

Laughing, the Monk observed, "I've already granted you the right to sit in my Dharma-seat, but circumstances are still not ripe for your accession!"

I prostrated myself in acknowledgement of these momentous words, feeling deep shame.

Mustering contributions

The retreat ended on the first day of the eighth month. Afterwards, the Monk was invited to transmit the precepts on Mount Baizhu in Taiping prefecture. That retreat began on the first day of the ninth month and concluded on the

---

328. literally, the Port Great Temple. It may have been an imperial monastery.

eighth day of the tenth month. Afterwards, we returned to Mount Baohua. Our next ordination retreat took place at the Bao'en Wanfo Pavilion in Nanjing. It began on the first day of the tenth lunar month and concluded on the eighth day of the second month.

On the twelfth day, I announced that I would take a leave of absence in order to muster rice donations. Just outside the north gate of Jurong county[329] lay a meditation studio. It was the abode of Master Xuechuang, who was originally from Changshu. Although he had never taken the precepts, he and I were on excellent terms. As soon as he heard that I was out collecting rice donations, he energetically stepped in to assist me. In less than half a month, we had mustered over three hundred bushels of rice; moreover, through his mediation, denizens of the local villages agreed to transport the rice up to Mount Baohua by the first month of the new year.

When I returned to the mountain, I had a formal interview with the Monk and brought him up-to-date on the outcome of my alms collection campaign.

Upon hearing the news, the old fellow beamed at me and said, "It appears that your fund-raising karma is excellent. Those without the proper causal foundation would never have succeeded as you have."

Early in the second month, a squire from the He Commandery of Suzhou requested that the Monk conduct a precept transmission at the Beichan Temple. That ordination retreat was over on the eighth day of the fourth month, whereupon we returned to Mount Baohua.

---

329. in modern Jiangsu province

Enforcing Buddhist regulations

The collapse of the Ming dynasty in 1644

During the seventeenth year of the Chongzhen regnal era, on the fifteenth day of the seventh lunar month, the civil and military ministers of Nanjing held an ordination assembly to commemorate the recently-deceased Chongzhen Emperor.[330] The Monk was invited to preside on the ordination platform and transmit the precepts. The newly-instated Hong'guang Emperor[331] dispatched Qiao Shang, an imperial eunuch from the inner court, to present the Monk with a purple robe and a bolt of golden silk fabric. The retreat concluded on the fifteenth day of the tenth month, whereupon we returned to Baohua.

Strictly enforcing Buddhist regulations

In the middle of the tenth month, the Da'neng'ren Temple, which was located in Shaoxing prefecture in central Zhejiang, invited the Monk to hold an ordination retreat that would start on the fifteenth day of the twelfth lunar month. The Prince of Lu[332] took refuge and frequently came to listen to Dharma talks. The *yiyou* year (1645) heralded the first year of the Hong'guang regnal era.[333] This ordination

---

330. On the 25th of April, 1644, the Chongzhen Emperor committed suicide after Li Zicheng's rebel army invaded and overturned the central government in Beijing. Afterwards, Ming loyalists proclaimed the Southern Ming dynasty in Nanjing, which lasted until the city surrendered to Qing Manchu forces on 8 June, 1645.

331. The Hong'guang Emperor Zhu Yousong (1607–1646) ruled the Southern Ming from 1644 to 1645. In 1646, he was captured and executed by Qing forces.

332. Zhu Yihai (1618–1662) had been invited to come to Shaoxing in 1645 by Ming loyalist leaders. There, he was enfeoffed as the prince regent, but was forced to flee when the Qing conquered Zhejiang. His grave has been discovered in Kinmen, a group of islands belonging to Taiwan. The Lu fiefdom was originally located in Yanzhou prefecture.

333. Although the Prince of Fu was crowned as the Hong'guang emperor

The Rambling Story of a Dream

assembly was over on the tenth day of the second month in the year 1645.

After the Shaoxing retreat, we were invited to the Three Pagodas Temple in Jiaxing. En route, we forded the Qiantang River, and then lodged at the Shaoqing Temple. While we were there, the Prince of Lu[334] took reliance, along with his entire prefectural retinue. He invited the Monk to mount the ancient ordination platform of the Shaoqing Temple and transmit the precepts. Since the Monk had already accepted the invitation of the Jiaxing Three Pagodas Temple, the Shaoxing ordination had to be postponed until the previously-scheduled assembly was concluded.

We arrived at the Three Pagodas Pavilion on the twenty-eighth day of the second lunar month. The transmission assembly began on the first day of the third month. Over five hundred novices attended, half of whom were from the Tiantong Temple. I made sure that Buddhist regulations were stringently enforced. Every novice studied the Vinaya conscientiously; not a single one of them dared to disregard the meditation hall rules.

I plan to have a stūpa erected in recognition of the Monk's benevolence.

One day, it suddenly struck me how quickly the Monk had recalled me from my retreat on Mount Huang. He had issued a compassionate order enjoining me to return

---

on June 19, 1944, his reign officially began in the next lunar year. This was the Hong'guang regnal era.

334. Zhu Changfang (1608–1646) surrendered to the Qing dynasty in Beijing and was executed. His title contains a different 'lu' character and is distinct from the previous fiefdom.

Erecting a stūpa

to Baohua. Grateful for his benevolence, I decided to have a stūpa erected to ensure him felicity and longevity. My plan would also provide me with a pretext for avoiding Mount Baohua: it would enable me to pursue personal cultivation in a location unalloyed by the monastery's state of moral laxity.

I went to the abbot hall and prostrated myself before the Monk, then presented a formal report elucidating my project. The Monk gave his permission gladly.

I immediately set to work, hanging up a scroll on which my own name with my contribution of one hundred silver taels figured prominently at the top of the list. Underneath, space was provided for each class of novices[335] to add their names and donations. I explained the project to them and told them that their contributions could be large or small, according to their means. Hearing my speech, everyone was inspired with filial piety and made a donation. In all, over three hundred taels were raised during the retreat.

On the twentieth day of the fifth month, we heard a rumor that the Qing army would be crossing the river on the eighteenth. Nanjing had already surrendered to Manchu forces. The Monk ended the retreat immediately and went back to Suzhou.

Wuxie,[336] a bhikṣuṇī from Liangshan county,[337] had been tonsured and ordained by the Monk. When she got the news that the Monk had arrived in Suzhou, she came to escort

---

335. Novices training for ordination were divided into as many as six classes, each of which was assigned to its own hall. Like meditation halls, these spaces accommodated sixty or seventy people, who lived and slept there for the duration of an ordination retreat.
Holmes Welch, *The Practice of Chinese Buddhism*, 287.
336. 'Never-resting'
337. *Huyện Lương Sơn* lies in northern Vietnam.

The Rambling Story of a Dream

him to Liangshan.[338] The Tanhua Pavilion[339] in Liangshan county was the patriarchal hall of the Tiantai sect, which was the Monk's own lineage. Due to his close ties with the region, the Monk visited it frequently; hence, many local residents had taken reliance under his wing.

When I told Wuxie of my plan to erect a longevity stūpa in honor of Sanmei, she promptly donated one hundred taels herself, and then proceeded to muster over four hundred taels for the project. At this point, the alms donations totaled nine hundred seventy-six taels, five mace.[340]

With the country in a state of chaos, it was hard to find anyone trustworthy to take custody of the donations, so I had to assume the responsibility myself. I had to carry that bundle of cash with me wherever I went. You can imagine what an encumbrance it was!

Sanmei is taken ill and returns to Baohua.

Jiechu, the rector of the Ganlu[341] hermitage in Huqiu,[342] deferentially received the Monk as a guest, hoping to give the elderly master a chance to rest. Early in the sixth month, the Monk was afflicted by splenasthenic diarrhea.[343] There was no way to get him back to Baohua—soldiers were everywhere and water routes had become impassable. The

---

338. Perhaps three thousand refugees from Ming China fled to Vietnam. The intention here might have been to get Sanmei out of the country.

339. built during the Southern Song by Prime Minister Jia Sidao (1213–1275). It was affiliated with the Tiantai sect.

340. 10 mace (*qian*) equaled one silver *tael*.

341. 'Sweet Dew'

342. in modern Suzhou

343. Relegated to the spleen in traditional Chinese medicine, this illness was characterized by weakness, cold extremities, and lack of appetite.

Sanmei is taken ill

band of followers that accompanied the Monk on his travels gradually dispersed. Only Master Xiangxue and I stayed with him, along with his attendants, his secretary, and some other staff members. Fourteen people stayed at the hermitage to serve him. Hearing the news that Sanmei was ailing, newly-ordained disciples at the Yaofeng Temple came to escort him to their temple so that he could be nursed back to health. After we arrived there, his condition worsened. I was deeply troubled.

A few days later, Master Xiangxue, too, announced his departure and left us. One day, we got word that Qing forces had already reached the town of Mudu,[344] which was not far from the Yaofeng Temple. Everyone at the temple fled to evade the approaching danger. I persuaded the Monk to go to the mountaintop with me and take shelter.

During the first weeks of the sixth lunar month, news came that the roads were passable, and the Monk bade me find a boat to take us back to Mount Baohua.

When we got to Changzhou, our passage was blocked by Qing soldiers, and we were forced to go back to Suzhou. After three or four days, things had settled down somewhat, so once again, we hired a boat and sailed to Xinfeng town, only to see that the stretch of river upstream was crowded with boats that were turning back around and sailing towards us. We asked the boat passengers what was going on.

They told us: "The Qing forces have already invaded Zhenjiang prefecture and will be entering Danyang shortly. We're making a run for it. Your boat will never make it through!"

Thus, we had to turn around and go back to Suzhou once again to wait for the turmoil to subside. Once we could

---

344. in modern Jiangsu province

see boats plying their way back and forth on the river, we continued our voyage.

On the twenty-sixth day of the sixth month, we finally arrived at Mount Baohua. The monastery's great assembly came out to greet the Monk, paying their respects and inquiring after his health.

Smiling, the Monk answered them: "It's certainly peaceful back here, and if my trip was a bit chaotic, so what! Today, I am letting you all know: In three days' time, before a week is up, I will be liberated from all entanglements!"

At these words, everyone burst into tears.

The Monk told them: "The transition from life to death is illusory. There is no actual coming or going, so why are you crying?"

Erecting a stūpa and deciding on a suitable location

That evening, I requested the presence of every monastery official to act as witnesses. I unrolled the scroll containing the list of alms-givers and their contributions to the longevity stūpa. Then, I asked Master Yuegu[345] to announce each name and donation recorded on the scroll, while Master Huimu kept a precise running tally. The final sum came to nine hundred seventy-six silver taels and five mace. In the presence of the assembly, the money was handed over to the head of the business office,[346] Master Dazhao.

That night, I recalled that when the temple's spatial orientation[347] was first being realigned, the Monk had informed Master Dazhao that his remains were to be

---

345. 'Moon Valley'
346. *dangjia*
347. according to the science of Chinese geomancy, or *fengshui*.

Planning Sanmei's stūpa

interred behind the temple hall. But in my experience, none of the monasteries that had erected commemorative stūpas behind their main temple halls had flourished. Accordingly, I resolved to induce the Monk to pick a different location for his stūpa. The next day, I came to the abbot's hall and made a tactfully indirect attempt to reopen the topic for fresh discussion.

"We are all delighted that you have allowed us to build a longevity stūpa! Where would you like us to place it?"

The Monk returned, "You must have forgotten that I asked to have my tomb placed behind the great Buddha hall."

I countered, "I've heard that you once conferred with a *fengshui* expert on ley lines.[348] The geomancer maintained that there are three earth cycles. The great cycle will eventually cause a building or location to flourish, but only after a developmental period of one hundred twenty years has elapsed. The median cycle will generate prosperity after a wait of eighty years, and the minor cycle requires forty years of development before a location reaches its full potential.

"Now, the earth lines behind the great hall are inward-flowing ['dragons'], but if the associated earth cycle does not allow this incoming energy to progress freely, the temple will never flourish. Future generations will claim that the longevity stūpa is blocking the incoming earth energy, so your tomb will eventually have to be relocated.

"In order to ensure the temple's everlasting prosperity, it would be better to erect your stūpa at the dragon's head. If your stūpa flourishes, there will be an abundance of resident monastics; similarly, if the temple has a large population of monks, your stūpa will prosper accordingly."

---

348. earth energy lines

The Rambling Story of a Dream

After a lengthy pause, the Monk finally conceded: "Just as you say—the stūpa should be built at the dragon-head location."

While we were discussing the issue, Master Dazhao and the rector Huimu were standing nearby.

"Each of you elders has heard the Monk's words," I told them. "He has decided that rather than have his stūpa built behind the main hall, it will instead be built in front at the dragon-head location."

Sanmei confers the purple robe and Prātimokṣa[349] upon me.

On the first day of the intercalary sixth month, the Monk ordered his attendant to bring him an almanac.

After perusing it, he declared: "On the fourth day, between nine and eleven o'clock in the morning, I shall achieve nirvāṇa."

Immediately, the sound of gongs, drums, and sticks could be heard throughout the temple, calling all of the monks to congregate in the abbot's quarters.

The Monk announced, "Jianyue shall be the heir to my Dharma seat."[350]

He then conferred upon me the purple robe and Prātimokṣa, saying, "With these objects, I command you to uphold the Three Disciplines of morality, meditation, and wisdom[351] tirelessly and expound the radiant precepts."

Kneeling before him, I declared, "Your humble servant is

---

349. the Buddhist precept manual

350. Although Zen abbotships were determined by enlightenment transmission, Baohua's abbots were the foremost Vinaya disciples of their predecessors.

351. *śīla*, *samādhi*, and *prajñā* [Skt]

Sanmei passes on the abbotship

the least capable monk in the entire temple. My ordination took place not long ago, and both my spiritual practice and accumulated merit are tenuous. I entreat you to confer this position upon your master ācāryas! I would willingly act as an auxiliary leader."

The Monk promptly turned his face inward and lay down without uttering a word.

I decided to go along with him temporarily, saying, "Your humble servant accepts your compassionate order. I'll take care of things for the time being. Once your Dharma body is in its eternal resting place, I will duly hand this position over to a proper abbot."

At these words, the Monk turned his face towards me, saying, "This was not a spur-of-the-moment decision—it has always been in my heart to name you as my Dharma heir. No more refusals!"

I accepted Sanmei's command and rose.

To Master Duxing, the Monk said, "You have amassed substantial virtue and have been a monk for many years. You shall serve as the karman preceptor.[352] You are qualified to maintain high standards for future generations of Buddhist students."

He then addressed Master Dazhao:[353] "You will continue to act as the monastery superintendent and assist Jianyue."

On the fourth day of the month, the Monk ordered the entire assembly to convene in the abbot hall. Water was drawn and he bathed.

---

352. *jiemo*

353. Hongyi comments, "Master Dazhao was a stable practitioner, although rather lacking in courage, vigor, and understanding. However, in comparison to Xiang Ācārya, who was unscrupulous, devoid of Way-mind, and heedless of the gracious trust that had been conferred upon him, Dazhao was by far the better candidate."

The Rambling Story of a Dream

He told the assembled monks, "As soon as this water has dried, I will be gone. Don't waste any time trying to fathom the mystery of my passing. There's no need to wear mourning clothes and weep. You are not allowed to broadcast an obituary. Do not hold any mundane rituals in my honor. After three days have passed, inter my remains at the temple's dragon mount."[354]

Having spoken his final commands, he ordered the congregation to chant the Buddha's name.[355] As soon as the water dried, sitting cross-legged in the lotus pose, he smiled and passed away.

Sanmei's physical body was enshrined in the Buddha hall,[356] and all of his commands were observed. For three days, everyone chanted sūtras with utmost sincerity. When three days had passed, the Buddhist assembly came bearing fragrant flowers and banners to escort the Monk to the dragon mount. He was enshrined in a stūpa built to house his intact earthly remains.

I couldn't bear it and had to retreat to my quarters. My intention was to spend three years as the stūpa attendant so that I could keep Sanmei's tomb swept and clean. I would use reed mats to protect the top from the elements and would chant scriptures night and day to commemorate the Monk's profound benevolence.

But my vow could only be kept for a month. The assembly forced me to return to the temple and installed me in the abbot's chamber.

---

354. *longshan*: in *fengshui*, the most auspicious location
355. *Namo Amitābha*: "I place my reliance on *Amitâbha* Buddha," a Pure Land chant.
356. Sanmei was not cremated: *roushen* signifies a mummified body. Many *roushen* are on public display in Buddhist monasteries.

Ten statutes

Circumstances spur me on to a higher level of spiritual attainment.

At the time of the Monk's passing, Xiang Ācārya was in Suzhou. He was deeply aggrieved that Sanmei had transmitted the robe and Prātimokṣa to me. From Suzhou, he travelled by boat upstream with the intention of going to the Chu region; he planned on getting there via Longtan and bypassing Baohua. Only after Master Dazhao sent him a personal letter entreating him to return did he come back to Mount Baohua and pay his respects at Sanmei's stūpa.

Having venerated the shrine, he hired artisans to engrave the *Śūraṅgama guan zhu*,[357] which he had compiled himself, in the Great Compassion Hall.[358] The workers made a mess of the place, so I suggested that it would be preferable for Master Xiang to have the work done in an outlying wing of the main building.

He retorted: "If you think that engraving a sūtra in this hall is dirty, what will you do in the future, when every room is vacant and you are all alone? When dust has accumulated everywhere and buildings are concealed by dense thickets of weeds? Who will be there to keep you company and clean up for you then?!!"

I replied austerely: "Master Xiang, before you make any more rash statements, please bear in mind that there are heavenly dragons and devas abiding here eternally, along with our illustrious ancestors. How could these guardians ever allow our monastery to fall into ruin?! And it is not necessary, Master Xiang, for you to waste time worrying about the future condition of your humble servant!"

---

357. *guanzhu*: "string of pearls"
358. the *Avalokiteśvara* Hall, in honor of Guanyin Bodhisattva

The Rambling Story of a Dream

Once this exchange was over, I went back to the abbot's chamber and gave the matter careful consideration. Rather than sigh mournfully over that unseemly conflict, I began to feel happy. Seen from another perspective, Master Xiang's irate words were a stimulus to put me on my mettle and spur me on to greater spiritual mastery. By addressing this challenge, my intention, willpower, and determination to uphold the Dharma-gate would become firmer. I decided that stricter rules must be put in force immediately; corrupt practices must be rooted out; Buddhist regulations must be stringently upheld.

That night, I drafted ten statutes. The next day, I convened the entire assembly and sent respectful invitations to the two elders, Xiangxue and Dazhao.

Addressing the group, I declared: "Your humble servant's monastic comportment is inferior and my blessings are paltry. I am only leading this monastery because the Monk commanded me to do so.

"Now, I have formulated ten statutes that are unlike those governing any other Way-place.[359] I have invited these two senior monks to act as witnesses while I announce the new regulations to the saṃgha.

"***One***: In ancient temples, one frequently sees residents lighting stoves for themselves. Everyone does just as they please. Such Buddhist halls always remain silent and empty. Rarely does one see monastics engaged in intense spiritual practice there. Under these circumstances, Buddhist monasteries have become decadent.

"The problem is due to lax temple leaders who don't distinguish between those who are only along for the ride and aspirants who sincerely wish to embark on the path

---

359. *daochang*

to enlightenment. They tonsure anyone and transmit the precepts to all comers, regardless of their suitability for the monastic life.

"Now, it is my intention to ensure that Mount Baohua will flourish forever. I intend to put an end to the scourge of undisciplined temple residents. The kāṣāya and the Dharma should exist together harmoniously. For the time being, we will not tonsure any Buddhist aspirants here.

"*Two*: One often sees monks hoarding money in order to support themselves in old age. Even young temple residents do this. Such monks are unwilling to practise spiritual refinement—they just sit around shamelessly, and their slack behavior infects the entire assembly. In the end, almsgivers and Dharma protectors will look askance at their hypocrisy: the radiance of the Buddha-gate will be lost.

"We of Mount Baohua must root out such cynical behavior and practices. Elderly spiritual practitioners shouldn't have to hoard money for themselves. They can continue to live in the temple and let the karmic conditions governing their lives unfold."[360]

"*Three*: Temples commonly elect an alms-master whose job it is to meet with donors, muster contributions, keep a register of all donations, and publicize the contents of the

---

360. Ven. Hongyi quotes two analogous passages here to support the point: "The Buddhist Canon states, 'Practise the Way single-mindedly and adhere to the Dharma in all activities without concern for practical necessities like clothing or food.' The Tathāgata emitted a ray of light from the tuft of white hair between his eyebrows (*ūrṇā* [Skt]). Among the boundless (*niyuta* [Skt]) rays of wisdom that shone out, an inexhaustible portion is supplied to all Buddhist disciples who have renounced the world.

"'A person of integrity seeks the Way scrupulously, without any concern for the practical benefits that this pursuit might yield.'" [The Confucian Analects] The commentator notes dismissively, "If this saying applies to people in the mundane world [i.e., Kong Qiu], it is even more relevant to those who have gone forth from secular life."

alms register. The abbot plies potential donors with streams of effusive compliments in order to cultivate lay patrons and trap them into making lavish contributions. Other monastery officials are even more prone to ingratiating themselves with benefactors. The alms-master eventually starts taking personal credit for all temple donations, deceiving the assembly and monopolizing temple management. Such unrighteous causes yield evil results: almsgivers will lose faith in Buddhist monks and stay away from the temple.

"At Baohua, we will no longer appoint an alms master, nor will we publicize the contents of our donation ledger. We will let grains and other contributions arrive as they list. Genuine spiritual practitioners never go hungry.

"**Four**: As soon as an elder monk is awarded the title of abbot, he has a small kitchen installed for his personal use, accumulates a store of fruit and other delicacies, orders his own food and drink, and indulges in private feasts. Those who are in the abbot's good graces can enjoy a share of this bounty, but no one else gets a taste.

"A monastery leader ought to be ashamed to hold such a lofty title, all the while disregarding the responsibility that such a position entails. A monk who treats members of the assembly unequally is an abbot in name only.

"Although a place in the refectory is always reserved for the abbot, he seldom deigns to put in an appearance. Now, your humble servant will be taking all three meals of porridge with the assembly, and any delicacies that come my way shall go directly to the storehouse.

"When alms-givers or Dharma protectors come to visit the mountain, they will certainly be treated with hospitality; however, showing courtesy to guests doesn't count as a sign of partiality.

Ten statutes

"***Five***: Every temple officer[361] that is involved in functions for lay people is entitled to a share of the donations that accrue. Gratuities for commemorative death rites[362] are received in the abbot hall, while vegetarian food donations go to the treasury.[363] That is known as dividing revenues into two separate channels.

"If a benefactor only gives incense money for a private ceremony, certain resident monks will be placed in charge of hospitality. If the presiding monks keep believers' monetary contributions for themselves, how will the business office manager be able to afford the seven commodities (oil, salt, firewood, rice, wine, vinegar, and tea)? How does that accord with the principle: 'What belongs to the resident monks belongs to me; my money and possessions are the property of every temple resident.'?

"Now, I have yet to acquire enough merit to attain full enlightenment, but in the meantime, I intend to root out this sordid practice. All of the incense money received by the temple will be common property. If someone draws on these funds for private purposes, it must be announced to the entire assembly.

"***Six***: In every location where a precept transmission will be held, posters are put up in advance to announce the allotted time of three to seven days or a month. The attendees are all required to pay a fee for their platform space. Afterwards, when the assembly is over, every attendee is sent out with a donations

---

361. *tangtou*

362. Such rites could entail special equipment, a feast for the monks, and fees for every monk who presides at the event.

363. Both branches of the monastery administration had their own accountants. The business office handled stores of food, as well as the temple's permanent property (*changzhu*). The abbot's compound, too, had its own accountant and revenues.

register.³⁶⁴ Such registers are only business expedients—they have nothing to do with promulgating the Dharma.

"From now on, when participants come to us requesting ordination, Mount Baohua will not exact platform fees from them. When leaving the temple, no one will receive a donations register. We will no longer use Dharma transmission retreats as sources of profit; rather, we shall let time and circumstance provide what they will. In purity, we will transmit the precepts.

"***Seven***: In every famous monastery and shrine, the quarters for temple officers are stocked with private stores of tea and delicacies and lavishly furnished with antiques and curios. Groups of people gather there, sitting and chatting together. Besides wasting time in idleness, they freely gossip and discuss the good and bad points of others, which prompts temple residents to start judging some monks as being better than others.

"This idle practice causes more harm than good. How can we shamelessly enjoy the support of believers this way! Hence, I am now abolishing the practice. Any saṃgha member who is living here in harmony and has Way-friends coming to visit or acquaintances who are running errands here has the right to bring them to a guest chamber and treat them hospitably. Thus, we will not be shown wanting in cordiality to visitors, and the temple will enjoy a brilliant reputation.

"***Eight***: It is customary for monastery officials to respond to joyous or sad events³⁶⁵ that occur in lay peoples' lives with suitable congratulations or condolences. They give the laity money and other items as bribes with the intention

---

364. These registers were evidently fundraising ploys, making ordinands duty-bound to solicit alms for the monastery.

365. i.e., marriages or funerals

of currying favor with almsgivers. Such monks have left mundane life, yet they still participate in worldly ceremonies. Although they have renounced the world, they do not cherish the rules governing Buddhist monks and neglect to act with proper decorum. They covet profitable offerings. That is a grave violation of the Buddhist precepts.

"Now, owing to its remote location, Mount Baohua is far removed from the secular world. Additionally, the denizens of this temple all adhere to the Buddhist Vinaya and practise its tenets steadfastly. Noting how we refrain from participating in secular affairs, any benefactor who is a true believer will understand and approve of our dedication.

"**Nine**: Due to our isolated location, we must operate differently than temples located in convenient proximity to cities and towns. Everything that we need, such as firewood and rice, has to be carried manually up the mountain.

"From now on, transporting commodities up the mountain will be a communal job. A signal rattle[366] will be sounded to call the saṃgha together for work duty. If you yourself don't participate, yet you order others to get the job done for you, the saṃgha will not be in unity.[367]

"From now on, any time we do manual labor that involves descending the mountainside, your humble servant won't let others bear the brunt of the load—I won't just follow along behind. For any job involving manual labor, I will hunch my shoulders and get on with it. We will not force anyone who is in poor health to participate, and elderly monks will be exempt from work duty and can

---

366. a hollow wooden or bamboo stick

367. Every clause of these statutes follows the Vinaya exactly. For further information on the precepts for monks and nuns, see *The Buddhist Monastic Code*, an online translation with commentary by Geoffrey DeGraff.

rest. Henceforward, the entire monastic community will live and work together.

"***Ten***: Living within the same territory,[368] the great assembly must comply with Buddhist regulations. Any decorative, cherished object must be dispensed with. Monastics cannot wear silk fabrics, nor can they dress up and groom themselves like lay people. We must never be separated from our three robes, which must be dyed an unattractive color.[369] Everyone has a begging bowl; according to the Vinaya, these bowls should be made of clay or iron.

"No Prātimokṣa is read after the midday meal, so monastics must make an even greater effort to follow the Buddha's teachings during the afternoon and evening hours. We must encourage one another to practise our vows assiduously. If the assembly makes a concerted effort to uphold the precepts, even indolent monks will become more diligent.

"Today, I am establishing these ten clauses as the governing statutes of our monastery. With such lofty regulations in place, we can rest assured that our temple will flourish!"[370]

Master Dazhao voiced his reservations about the proposed statutes: "For the most part, these rules are probably viable; however, dispensing with an alms-master would be a grave error. As soon as we institute this policy, our supply lines will be permanently severed, and by the time we've realized our mistake, it will be too late to redress the error!"

---

368. Buddhist temples are built upon consecrated territories.

369. a dull yellowish-brown or grey color

370. "It is stated in a monastic code of rules: 'The more strictly the rules are applied, the more people there will be living in a monastery. The looser the rules, the fewer people.' This was partly because strictness attracted donations from the laity and partly because it would be impractical to have several hundred persons living together in disorder." Holmes Welch, *The Practice of Chinese Buddhism*, 1900–1950, 4.

Prohibiting private stoves

I countered, "It is true that your humble servant has only recently begun serving as the abbot—I certainly don't have the proper qualifications for such a position. But I vow that we will not follow the example of other monasteries. Such places are bustling with commerce; their gates are like marketplaces. I intend to emulate the austere practices of the ancients."

Master Xiang took in my words silently; then, he stalked haughtily out of the room. Master Da was visibly displeased. Heaving a sigh, he also retreated to his quarters.

The prohibition of private cooking stoves

While the Monk was still alive, three court eunuchs took reliance. Official Sun received the Buddhist name Dunwu,[371] Official Liu's Buddhist name was Dunxiu,[372] and Official Zhang was called Dunzheng.[373] When Prince Yu's[374] troops crossed the Yangtze River, these three eunuchs fled to Mount Baohua and begged for ordination. At the time, Sanmei was out on a mission, so Master Dazhao hung a portrait of the Monk in the central hall and tonsured all three of them.

By the time Sanmei got back to Baohua, each of the eunuchs had his own private chamber. On the thirtieth day of the ninth month, Liu Dunxiu had a secret conference

---

371. 'Sudden Enlightenment'
372. 'Sudden Practice'
373. 'Sudden Realization'
374. Prince Yu (Dodo) (1614–1649) belonged to an imperial Manchu clan. In 1645, he crossed the Yangtze River, took over Nanjing, the Southern Ming capital, and captured the Hong'guang Emperor. The same year saw the death of Sanmei and the installation of Jianyue as the abbot of Mount Baohua. Jianyue was 44 years old at the time.

The Rambling Story of a Dream

with Master Xiangxue and Master Dazhao. He wanted to have a small stove installed in his quarters. The two masters gave him the go-ahead.

On the first day of the tenth month, I was invited to take tea in Liu's chamber. The two senior monks were already seated there when I arrived. Dunxiu explained the proposed stove to me and told me that both Xiang and Da had already given their approval. At this point, they wished to introduce the project to the new abbot.

I told them, "Your humble servant is now the abbot. Why have you only brought the matter before me after all of you have talked it over and settled things secretly among yourselves? I should have been present at the discussion.

"I will now inform you of three things:

"**One**: During the former abbot's lifetime, no matter where the Monk was invited to hold an ordination, he always stipulated that if anyone installed a private stove and brought in pots or dishes, these items would have to be destroyed immediately. Everyone was expected to eat in the refectory. Sanmei would only hold a retreat if his rules were observed; otherwise, he refused to attend.

"Fewer than four months have passed since the Monk attained nirvāṇa. How dare you live with our resident monks yet install your own private stove?! You are deceiving the former abbot. Your actions are absolutely impermissible.

"**Two**: If you insist upon having your own stove, it will be over my dead body. After my death, perhaps you'll be free to indulge in lawless, disorderly conduct.

"**Three**: If karmic circumstances call me away from Baohua and I must relinquish the position of abbot, you can go along with whatever the senior monks decide. But

Strict adherence to Buddhist regulations

if I am in residence on this mountain, I will never allow our monastery to become lax and degenerate!"

Having said this, I shook out my sleeves and strode from the room. Masters Xiang and Da were left speechless; Dunxiu's face reddened with shame and disappointment. That incident marked the beginning of my campaign to revive and revitalize the Vinaya.

I insist upon strict adherence to Buddhist regulations.

One day, I convened the monastic assembly in the great shrine hall. Additionally, I requested the presence of the two masters Xiangxue and Dazhao.

After prostrating myself, I addressed the assembly: "Formerly, I served as an attendant at the seat of the former Monk. I worked together with every senior master to assist the Monk in his efforts to expound the Dharma. No matter what project was in the works, the former abbot was always careful to give the senior monks advance notice. I am now letting you know that I intend to modify a policy that has been in effect for quite some time.

"I once heard the Monk give this compassionate instruction: 'From the time of the Vinaya Patriarch[375] up to the present,' he said, 'in order to revitalize the Buddhist precepts and teachings, we have made use of expedient means that are cleverly designed to fit each situation and listener. But throughout our mission, it is always understood that our intention should never waver from the Vinaya. Only after we have successfully converted our lay audience do we introduce Buddhist discipline.'

---

375. Daoxuan (596–667)

The Rambling Story of a Dream

"Now, your humble servant bears the sole responsible for our ministry—the burden lies on my shoulders alone. It is clear to me that in order to inculcate the Vinaya, we must not only know its doctrine, but must also follow its rules! Now that I have made this proclamation before the assembly, you will be expected to adhere to Buddhist regulations and practice what you preach."

Three days after my speech to the monastic assembly, Master Dazhao relinquished his position as head of the business office, Dunwu expressed a wish to serve as a superintendent,[376] and Master Xiangxue went to the Tian'ning Temple in Changzhou to lecture on the scriptures. All of my Haichao hermitage ordination brothers scurried off in search of brighter prospects. Around ninety percent of the officials in charge of the various departments and training halls left the temple.

Those who— (1) were unable to carry out our mission in compliance with the Vinaya, (2) couldn't embrace a life of poverty and simplicity with equanimity, and (3) were unable to participate in work parties to convey supplies up the mountain—were free to leave. I didn't bother trying to persuade anyone to stay.

Over a hundred comrades remained willingly at the temple. These monks worked diligently and made a concerted effort to help and encourage one another. Their common goal was to uphold the precepts.

---

376. *jianyuan*

Chanting the boundaries

**I chant the boundaries to establish a territory.
We hold an ordination with three people on
the platform at once.**

In the middle of the tenth month, over thirty people begged for ordination. This group was hosted by Longsha[377] of Yancheng county.[378] In preparation for the event, I first announced the boundary markers to the saṃgha and established an ordination territory.[379] Having established the territory, we held an ordination wherein three people at once received the full precepts on one platform.[380, 381]

Master Dazhao and his Way-friends never uttered a word to my face about it, but after descending the platform, they were overflowing with negative comments. They said that I had been commanded by the former Monk to carry on in his footsteps, but now, I'd gone ahead and made radical alterations to his legacy by changing our original ordination procedure. They averred that in the past, chanting the

---

377. 'Dragon Sand': probably a temple. The only available reference to Longsha Temple is to be found in the Ming-Qing-era poet Su Sheng's idyllic seven-character quatrain.

378. Salt City county

379. Like many transactions mentioned in the text, this is a formal saṃgha-karman.

380. Ordaining three people on one platform: Previously, nine people at once could receive the full precepts at Baohua. After consulting the Vinaya, Jianyue revised the practice to three ordinands at once. Ven. Jianyue mentioned this practice in his work: *The Orthodox Procedure for Triple-Platform Precept Transmission (San tan chuan jie zheng fan)*, 1660. Jinyü Wen, *"Jianyue laoren sixiang yanjiu"* in *Fojiao daohang*, 4/12/2009. https://www.fjdh.cn/wumin/2009/04/07210350873.html

381. Another innovation was the Triple-Platform ordination rite, in which the bodhisattva precepts, the novice precepts, and full ordination were conferred during the same ceremony, or after a short interval of time had elapsed. Hsuan-Li Wang, "Gushan: The Formation of a Chan Lineage during the Seventeenth Century and its Spread to Taiwan," PhD diss., Columbia University, 2014, p. 110, note 295.

The Rambling Story of a Dream

perimeter to establish a territory was seldom done; moreover, ordaining groups of three people at once was unheard of. They criticized me for violating the code of filial piety.

I knew that this flurry of criticism was due to the monks' lack of familiarity with the Vinaya, so I simply brushed the matter off and pretended not to have heard their grumbling.

One day, when Master Dazhao happened to stroll into the abbot's quarters,[382] I tactfully broached the subject, saying, "If you ever have some free time, why not read the Vinaya section of the Buddhist canon? It might be a way of amusing yourself when you have nothing else to do. How about it?"

He took my advice and perused the entire section of the Buddhist canon pertaining to moral discipline.[383] Belatedly, he discovered that the procedure I'd followed during the disputed ordination was quite legitimate. He came back to my chamber to have a word with me privately and expressed effusive admiration for my judgement. After that, the controversy over the Yancheng ordination was dispelled without the necessity of my issuing a formal prohibition.

I purchase a field in order to dispel murderous rancour.

In the days when Liu Dunxiu was still an imperial eunuch, he had given Sun Dunwu four hundred silver taels and told him to go and purchase some property near the temple's administrative wing. Liu's intention was to use its revenues to support himself in old age. Dunwu was negligent in carrying out Liu's instructions. He squandered the money on

---

382. The abbot's quarters constituted a separate unit in the monastery in which the abbot's equipment, monetary funds, and attendants were housed.

383. Vinaya-piṭaka [Skt]

The local peasants revolt

a piece of infertile ground with insufficient acreage. Due to poor soil and lack of space, the sharecroppers' plots of land did not yield enough grain to pay their rent.

Liu Dunxiu was furious. He concealed a sharp axe in his robes with the intention of hacking Dunwu to death. Seeing that a heinous crime was about to be committed, everyone was horrified and panicked. Master Dazhao conveyed the news to me. I told him that as soon as catastrophe erupted outside our walls, it would infect the nearby administrative wing with its poison.

Fortunately, there was still money left over from the stūpa building project. I decided to utilize this remainder to resolve the grievance between the two monks. I purchased the piece of land as a real estate investment that would fund incense and candles for the shrine. Mollified, Dunxiu lowered the price by a hundred taels. Thus, the administration hall reverted to a state of tranquility.

Bannermen set their horses loose in the fields and incite the peasants to revolt.

In the third year of the Shunzhi regnal era,[384] bannermen[385] set their horses loose to graze in peasants' wheat fields. Not knowing what was going on, the villagers confiscated the horses. In retaliation, General Abatai[386] ordered his soldiers to capture the villagers, who were thought to be rebels. Most of the peasants were killed; their wives and property were confiscated by officials. Those who managed to escape

---

384. 1646: The Shunzhi Emperor (r. 1644–1661) was the second ruler of the Qing dynasty. Jianyue was forty-five years old.

385. Manchu armies and households were organized into eight banners.

386. Prince Abatai (1589–1646) was a Manchu general.

abandoned their families and fled. It was impossible to return to their homes, so they were forced to scatter into the surrounding countryside.

A few leaders suddenly emerged from among the beleaguered peasants. They organized the fugitives into a rebellious mob under the pretext of helping them to redress their grievances. Unfortunately, by inciting a mass revolt, the crowd-mongers were only bringing further affliction upon the honest villagers.

Master Dazhao was terrified. Leading his Dharma brothers,[387] he fled down the mountain.

A retreat kept in strict purity

Early in the fourth month, it occurred to me that although bandits were still causing trouble, the temple should nevertheless hold a varṣa retreat with pravāraṇā.[388] For too long, we had been lax about holding a rains retreat in compliance with the Buddha's teachings. I had only recently become abbot and was insisting that the monastery follow the Buddhist code to the letter. The time for the summer retreat was upon us, so it couldn't be put off any longer.

Therefore, the retreat began on the sixteenth day of the fourth month. Over one hundred sixty bhikṣus attended, as well as eight śrāmaṇeras. A total of one hundred seventy-three people came to the retreat, all of whom adhered strictly to Buddhist rules and practised diligently. They were twice as conscientious as those who had attended previous retreats.

---

387. elder disciples of the same teacher

388. A repentance ceremony (*pravāraṇā*) is held to conclude the summer rains retreat (*varṣa*).

Snaring a rebel collaborator

To avert calamity, we snare a rebel collaborator.

When the twentieth day of the fifth month arrived, before dawn, the bandit chief Zhang Xiufeng led a band of over a hundred strong to our gates.

As soon as the monastery gates were opened, the rabble swarmed in and announced: "You have many buildings in this monastery compound and a large cooking area. We're going to use your facilities for a few days."

I countered: "You can use some of our rooms and our kitchen stove, but two things will be inconvenient for us to accommodate. One: You go about demanding that people hand over cash to you. If they refuse, you capture them, hang them up, torture them, and interrogate them. We monks would be here witnessing your cruelty, which would be awkward for both sides. Two: We would be eating with you from the same pot. If government officials find out, we'd suffer mass extermination for collusion with enemies of the dynasty.

"I've heard that when this temple was first being built by Grandmaster Miaofeng,[389] local village elders and townsfolk came forward enthusiastically to labor as construction workers. The job of transporting brick, tile, wood, and rock for the bronze pavilion was also done with the help of those meritorious fathers and grandfathers. Now, if you lay waste to their virtuous contributions, our own field of blessings will be spoilt, as well.

"All in all, there are lots of places outside the monastery where you can stay. Go and seek lodgings elsewhere!"

I adamantly refused them four times in this manner,

---

389. Miaofeng Fudeng (1540–1613) was a master builder who enjoyed the patronage of Empress Dowager Li during the Wanli era.

The Rambling Story of a Dream

until Zhang Xiufeng finally backed down: "All right, we'll do as you say. We'll camp outside the monastery."

Much to our surprise and dismay, we found out that the monk Kexiu had an older brother who was a bandit chief. As it happened, his brother belonged to the band that had just come to our gates. Kexiu went out frequently to visit his relative. When I asked him about their movements, he refused to utter a word. Although the monastic assembly was in a state of apprehension and alarm, Kexiu wasn't the least bit concerned.

I ordered the saṃgha: "Each one of you must bring a piece of firewood here; we will burn Kexiu alive. By getting rid of him, we'll dispel calamity and preserve our community's abiding peace."

As soon as Kexiu got wind of the plan, he was scared witless. He locked the door of his room tightly and refused to come out. Kexiu's mentor Jixian came to me in tears.

Kneeling before me, he implored me to set some conditions whereby the miscreant could be released: "What can be done to save my disciple's life?"

He immediately had Kexiu brought before me.

I told him, "Tomorrow at noon, the monastic residents will give a vegetarian meal. We will invite ten of the rebel chiefs, but absolutely no more than ten. If the bandits follow these instructions exactly, Kexiu's life will be spared. If too many people come, or nobody comes, the punishment will be carried out."

That evening, I convened the saṃgha and set forth a course of action for the banquet.

"Tomorrow at noon, when the bandit chiefs arrive, the temple residents will form themselves into two lines on the right- and left-hand sides of the room. Young monks will be stationed in front, while older monks will stand at the back of the line. You mustn't be afraid; no talking is allowed. If I haven't told you to go, you must continue to stand in your places without moving. When I say, 'Go,' you will all retire together, with the exception of twenty people: only they will remain at the banquet. Two people will be assigned to each place to act as attendants."

At noon, ten chiefs attended the meal as instructed. Once they were seated, the monks formed themselves into two rows.

I addressed the gathering, "You have been causing trouble because you have deep grievances to redress. Your wives and families have been taken captive, your fields and property have been confiscated by Qing officials. You are all Ming loyalists—of course, it is impossible for you to endure such wrongs. You've banded together as a last resort to save your families."

Hearing my words, the guests told me with tears in their eyes, "Master, you truly understand our plight."

At this, I rose half-way from my seat and bent forward, striking the table with my hand.

I declared, "You have been invited to attend this vegetarian feast today because the temple's bronze pavilion was built by Ming imperial order. The Dragon Canon[390] was published

---

390. The Tibetan Dragon Canon is a Qing-era text. Jianyue gave this speech in 1646, which predates the canon's publication. His autobiography, however, was composed in 1674.

Jianyue may have been cognizant of the Buddhist canon's direct line of transmission from earlier Tibetan texts to several woodblock editions that were commissioned by Ming imperial rulers. The 1605 Wanli edition was printed from the same blocks as the 1410 Yongle edition, which in turn was derived from the Tibetan *tshal pa* (Eastern) compilation. Scholars infer that the Qing "Dragon" edition (1669) was copied from the 1605 Ming canon.

Hence, despite the chronological confusion, Jianyue's speech is still credible: Ming-dynasty rulers did provide the foundation for the Qing-era Dragon Canon.

under the devout auspices of the Ming emperor. However, your presence here is preventing our monastic assembly from conducting our spiritual practice in tranquility. And how can we tolerate having our thousand-year-old abode of peace ruined! We have no choice but defend our temple!"

At my fiery words, the rebels were disconcerted and said repeatedly, "Understood, understood! Clearly, the monks of this temple are masters of literature and military strategy, too. Master, please do not get angry with us. Early tomorrow morning, we'll break camp and go somewhere else."

Once they had capitulated, I softened my tone to alleviate tension. The ten chiefs then took their leave and went out through the temple gate. Sure enough, just before dawn at the fifth night watch, they broke camp and departed.

But once it was daylight, we still had to worry about a sudden raid by Qing soldiers. I hurriedly ordered everyone to go out with lanterns and search the entire area in or around the temple. If they found any ashes from cooking fires, I instructed them to sweep the areas clean and cover them over with leaves; if any poultry or animals had been slaughtered, they were to pick up any leftover fur, feathers, and bones and toss everything into a deep mountain stream.

When the sun was about to rise, Lord Ma, a Qing regimental commander, led his troops up the mountain.

He rode his horse straight through the monastery gate and declared, "It has been ascertained that rebel bandits were living here for eight days. Why did you accommodate them without reporting them to the authorities?"

A. Hoh, *A newly acquired Tibetan Kanjur: The dragon tripitaka: 4 corners of the world* (The Library of Congress, 7/8/2016)

https://blogs.loc.gov/international-collections/2016/07/a-newly-acquired-tibetan-kanjur-the-dragon-tripitaka/

Snaring a rebel collaborator

I replied, "If it is true that they spent so much time here, they would certainly have left ashes from their cooking fires in the monastery grounds. They would also have slaughtered poultry and animals for food and left fur, feathers, and bones strewn about. Please have your men go out and look around carefully. That way, you'll know for certain whether or not your information is correct."

Accordingly, he ordered his men to comb the precincts for signs of a rebel camp. They came back and reported that no traces of rebel occupation had been found. At that, Lord Ma donated five silver taels to the monastery and took his leave.

From that time on, when almsgivers and believers heard announcements that officers and soldiers who guarded the pass were headed for the monastery, they made themselves scarce and stayed clear of the mountain. As a result, the temple received fewer donations and our three daily meals of thin gruel lacked oil and salt for several days. Bandits would sometimes come to the temple, which was a source of unease to those who were living together during the retreat.

I counselled the gathering, "We have just begun our retreat today. On no account should you succumb to fear and give up. Remember that there are always benevolent deities guarding over us unseen! Anytime Qing officials, soldiers, and cavalry or rebel bandits come to our gates, I will personally go out and deal with them. There's no need for you to trouble yourselves and get involved."

Hearing my words, the retreatants calmed down and were able to concentrate on their spiritual practice.

The Rambling Story of a Dream

We demolish temple buildings. Master Yuanyun composes a commemorative poem.

At the beginning of the sixth month, a mob of bandits came swarming up Mount Baohua. Some of them stayed at the Shangyuan ashram, some stayed at the Longwo[391] ashram, some stayed at the Huanghua Dong[392] ashram, some at the Lianxing Yan ashram, some stayed at the bridge pavilion, while others set up camp in the meditation hall behind the kitchen. These six locations lay within the monastery's administrative territory and were managed by our temple officials.

Some of the rebels wrote short notes informing us that they would be borrowing temple property, while others made use of military intimidation and summarily confiscated anything they wanted. Out of the entire temple population, only I came forth to deal with the invaders. I made clever use of expedient means and refused to give in to them.

Whenever word came that Qing officers and soldiers were coming, the rabble would scatter and leave us; as soon as they found out that the troops had gone, the bandits would regroup and come back. Giving the matter careful thought, I concluded that if the situation continued unchecked, great calamity would inevitably befall the temple. Whether the Qing army or the rebels invaded us, the outlook was equally grim. Hence, I mobilized the entire assembly and ordered the monks to demolish all of the buildings in which the rebels camped.

On the fifteenth day of the seventh month, I was in the abbot's quarters doing pravāraṇā.[393] The eminent monk

---

391. 'Dragon Nest'

392. 'Yellow Flower Cave': These are all Daoist terms used for esoteric meditation practices. These rooms might have been used as dormitories or as meditation rooms for lay Buddhists or hermits.

393. the repentance rite that concludes the summer rains retreat

A commemorative poem

Yuanyun, the west hall master,[394] composed a poem to commemorate the completed retreat.

> During this retreat, we've been practising single-mindedly in deep seclusion;
> Heeding the Buddha's strict regulations, we must bear any situation with hearts as impassive as cold ashes.

> During the time I've spent attending the rains retreat, this white-haired monk has been out wandering for less than a year;
> Now that the varṣa is over, those who've attended the Baohua Vinaya society's retreat delight in their renewed, refreshed lives.

> When receiving funds, Baohua adheres to the Southern assembly's ancient policies;[395]
> Meditating on rush mats, the judgements formulated in the Western lands[396] still hold.

> After pravāraṇā, there are fine words to utter:
> The Vinaya school of Upāli[397] roars like thunder.

---

394. The west hall (*xitang*) was a monastic of lesser importance whose status was comparable to that of any ordinary monastic seeking instruction. This was a person of proven virtue whose responsibilities included teaching and giving sermons. The west hall could also be a retired head priest from another monastery.

395. The ancient state called Funan was located near modern Cambodia. This country was converted to Buddhism very early; some of its monks brought Sanskrit texts to China.

396. *i.e.*, India

397. Upāli, one of the Buddha's ten outstanding disciples, was renowned as an expert on the Vinaya and pratimokṣa.

The Rambling Story of a Dream

One meal brings about the monastery's downfall.

By the beginning of the eighth month, the situation had calmed down somewhat. I entrusted the management of administrative affairs to Dunwu, the temple superintendent.[398] As for myself, I stayed in the abbot's building worshipping the Buddha.

On the twelfth day, I opened a window and looked outside: there was a middle-aged man hovering about the temple grounds. His upper garment was an old informal robe, perhaps that of a low-ranking civil servant; below that, vermillion cloth could be seen. He was pacing up and down in the corridor below me, scrutinizing everything around him.

Immediately, I went downstairs and told Dunwu, "That's a Qing soldier disguised as a commoner. He's here snooping around the temple. Don't let him stay here!"

Ignoring my command, Dunwu told the patrol guard in private, "That person is undergoing adversity. Let him stay with us for the Mid-Autumn festival. It will be an act of compassion!"

As soon as I found out what was going on, I summoned the patrol guard. When I rebuked him sharply for allowing the man to stay at the temple, he just raised his head and fixed me with an impenetrable stare.

After a short while, over a hundred bandits appeared, each one armed with a bamboo pole. They tightly surrounded the corridor, stationing themselves under the eaves of the building. Catching sight of the armed mob, Dunwu was petrified. He was an imperial eunuch: everyone knew that he was wealthy. Dunwu feared that the bandits would

---

398. *jianyuan*

seize the proceeds from his lavish salary, so he feigned cordiality and cooked rice for them hospitably, hoping to ingratiate himself with them.

As soon as I found out about this development, I immediately went downstairs. The bandits were already seated in the refectory with bowls and chopsticks placed before them in readiness for a meal. There didn't seem to be any way of getting rid of them.

I told Dunwu, "There are over a hundred temple residents here. Because of the meal that you are serving those bandits, our residents' lives and this thousand-year-old monastery will be annihilated. You are solely to blame for any disaster that befalls this community—I wash my hands of it."

Smiling, the man whose lower garments revealed vermillion fabric left the monastery. In fact, Qing forces had already set up camp atop Mount Dongxie. They had left the capital under the leadership of General Ba, the commanding officer; Lord Chen, who was the Yangtze River transport surveillance officer; and Lord Ao. Their mission was to annihilate rebel bandits.

Everyone finally realized that the smiling fellow who had been seen mysteriously slinking off was a spy from the Qing camp.

Qing troops close in on Baohua.

On the thirteenth day of the month, over a hundred Qing cavalrymen ascended Mount Baohua and tightly encircled Qianhua Temple in the middle of the night.[399]

---

399. Although the ancient temple situated in the Baohua (Precious Flower) hills is called 'Baohua' or 'Hua' throughout Jianyue's narrative, it had a succession of names during its existence. When it was built in the sixth century, it was called

The Rambling Story of a Dream

Everyone panicked, but there was no escape route.

When the sun came up, I told Dunwu, "I'm the abbot and you are the temple superintendent. The monastery is imperiled, so we must act together to save it. If Qing troops enter the temple compound, they'll seize every piece of temple property. The entire saṃgha will also be implicated."

Together, we opened the gate and went to the platform of the bronze pavilion.

The troop leader asked us, "Who are the two of you?"

I replied, "We're the abbot and the temple superintendent."

The military officer was pleased that we had come out of our own accord to give ourselves up. We all sat down together at the monastery gate. He wanted to know how many monks were living in the monastery.

I told him, "Including the elderly and the young, we have ninety-four people here."

The officer said, "Have them all brought out. We'll assume that anyone who doesn't come out must be a bandit."

Besides the monastics, there were also carpenters, bricklayers, tilers, and sculptors. Dunwu ordered all of them to come out and face the troops. The soldiers had brought along a captive bandit who was tightly trussed up. Now, they ordered him to point out his confederates among the people assembled.

The bandit was in a pitiable state. He had been locked up for twenty-four hours; he was crazed with fear and groggy with lack of sleep. He was incapable of speech—all that he could do was to nod his head confusedly. Due to

---

the Qianhua (Thousand Flower) Temple. During the Ming dynasty, it was rechristened Longchang (Abundance and Prosperity) Temple. During the Qing era, the main temple was renamed Huiju (Abiding Place of Wisdom) Temple. Here, Jianyue demonstrates his erudition.

his dazed, befuddled condition, when a carpenter came out and stood before him, he just nodded his head like an imbecile. One by one, sixteen people were falsely incriminated. They were shackled immediately. Each one of them had a rope tied around his neck and his hands fastened tightly behind his back. Six people remained; their necks were bound with rope and they were marched out together to the military camp.

The head officer saw that the monastery had been harboring lay people like the hapless workers and suspected that others might still be concealed on the premises. He ordered two military officers to lead four soldiers inside to investigate and commanded one soldier to secure the main gate. He ordered me and Dunwu to go into the temple with them.

Whenever they found a locked apartment, they would pierce its paper windows with their fingers and peer inside. So that they wouldn't suspect me of acting in collusion with the rebels, I demonstrated compliance by twisting the locks and snapping them off with my hands. I would then open the doors and let them look around. All that was to be seen were beds, and tables that were laden with scriptures. Several rooms were opened in this manner, revealing similar items. The soldiers were finally convinced that no further treachery lurked within our walls. Although a few more locked rooms remained, the officers didn't bother to have me destroy the locks.

The officers exited by the main gate and sat down.

They told me, "Someone reported that bandits were being concealed in this monastery. The grand lord commanded us to come here and seize them. These captives will be conveyed to the encampment under military escort.

Old or young, not a single one of them will get off lightly."

He immediately ordered a mounted soldier to bring up the rear of the convoy with one of the tethered monks in tow. The officer led the procession, marching me along with him.

I considered the situation: there was nobody remaining at the temple and the Qing soldiers were unsupervised. If the soldiers stationed at the rear decided to swarm into the temple, every last bit of temple property would be plundered.

Therefore, I offered a discreet suggestion: "When a military officer leads his troops out on an expedition, he is stationed in front to command his soldiers. When they return to the garrison, the officer stays at the back as a rear guard. I am the head of the monks, and you are in charge of the soldiers. You'd better command the soldiers who are leading the monks to go first, while the two of us bring up the rear. That way, no monks will escape, and the troops won't get disorderly."

Smiling, the military officer assented: "All right, just as you say!"

Daily spiritual practice brings us strength in adversity.

We marched for twenty *li*,[400] and finally reached the peak of Mount Dongxie. Entering the large encampment, we could see innumerable rebel bandits. Over a thousand villagers were incarcerated there, howling and wailing, naked and tightly bound. A soldier wielding a flag made all of us squat in one area and then made the sixteen falsely-accused artisans stand up. They were moved behind us and then made

---

400. over six miles

I don't relinquish monastic deportment

to squat down again.

From behind, we heard a soldier telling us, "All of you elders had better tell the truth; otherwise, you'll be treated just like these sixteen prisoners—beheaded!!"

No sooner had these words been uttered than—*clang*—all sixteen were killed. The six of us who remained were spared. Blood from the slaughtered villagers splattered everywhere, staining our robes.

I told the group of monastics, "Don't panic. Each of you, chant the Buddha's name single-mindedly. If we have formed this karma during multiple past lives, we will have to pay our debts today. If it is not our predestined fate to die here, we will naturally be liberated. Our constant spiritual practice will give us strength in adversity."

A muttering ensued as the monks all invoked the name of Amitābha[401] Buddha.

In the face of adversity, I don't relinquish monastic deportment.

District Magistrate Chen came down and ordered that Dunwu be brought out and tortured to obtain information. Dunwu confessed and told them that I was the abbot, so soldiers were sent to summon me. I reflected that life and death arise and disappear like bubbles floating on water. In any case, it behooved me to maintain the correct monastic demeanor in the face of adversity, so with a straight back, I walked up to them in a slow, composed manner. Two rows of soldiers stood at attention on the right and left, wielding sabers that were already drawn from their scabbards.

---

401. the buddha of infinite light and compassion

The Rambling Story of a Dream

Shouting in unison, they ordered me to kneel.

With a stern countenance, I declared, "As you can see, I am wearing the Tathāgata's kāṣāya. Buddhist regulations do not allow me to kneel before worldly people—how can I possibly kneel down and beg for my life to be spared? That would amount to willfully violating Buddhist law!"[402]

I stood bowing with my palms joined together during the interrogation, and then stood on the side. General Ba pointed at me and laughed. He touched his forehead and pointed upward with his thumb. In Manchurian speech, he conferred with General Ao and Lord Chen, the river controller.

An interpreter translated their conversation for me. "Grand Lord Ba says that the crown of your head is level with his own.[403] He says that you are a good monk. You don't have to kneel."

River Surveillance Officer Chen asked me, "Since there were bandits living on Mount Baohua for quite a while, why didn't you send a messenger out by night and report it to the authorities? Why did you take the liberty of concealing them?"

I replied, "Although Baohua is a lofty mountain, there is only a single road leading up and down its peak to accommodate travelers. If bandits come up on the front side of the mountain and descend via the back, those who observe them from the front would naturally lose sight of them and

---

402. Ven. Hongyi notes that Jianyue's voice was as loud and sonorous as an enormous temple bell.

403. Ven. Hongyi avers that the Manchu general was comparing the crown of his own head (or perhaps the peak of his pointed helmet) to Jianyue's topknot. The commentator also makes a far-fetched guess that both Jianyue and the general may have had fleshy knobs on top of their heads. Such features were seen as auspicious, since the Buddha is often depicted with a topknot [*uṣṇīṣa*, Skt]. One of the identifying marks of an enlightened being, the *uṣṇīṣa* has been construed as a fleshy knob on top of the head, perhaps covered with hairs that spiral upwards towards the sun.

I don't relinquish monastic deportment

think that they were occupying the mountain. Conversely, if the bandits ascend via the back road and descend by the front, those who watch them from the back of the mountain would also assume that they were camping on the mountain.

"That being the case, even if I went down the mountain and notified the authorities, they still wouldn't catch any bandits; moreover, I would be accused of supplying false information. The problem has nothing to do with my neglecting to report bandits or concealing them.

"Anyway, Mount Baohua is right before your eyes. Grand Lord, please examine the terrain yourself."

The river surveillance officer turned his head around and looked up at the mountain. As I had said, only one large road passed over the mountain.

Finally, he conceded, "There's no need for further investigation into this matter. Now, I want you to tell me about Imperial Eunuch Sun. He was an officer in the Ming inner court. He furnished clandestine support to rebel bandits and was secretly harboring treasonous thoughts. You must have known what he was up to."

I replied, "Imperial Eunuch Sun came to the mountain to become a monk in the sixteenth year of the Chongzhen regnal era. He has been acting as the temple superintendent for less than half a year now. All that I know about him is that he has relinquished his imperial title and is now practising spiritual cultivation. Whether, in his heart of hearts, he is good or evil—only he himself knows the answer to that question. How can I possibly discern what's going on in his mind?!"

The river surveillance officer acknowledged the soundness of my testimony: "Yes, I see that you wouldn't be able to ascertain his deepest secrets. Now, go!"

I left their presence just as I had entered, with a slow, composed tread.

A righteous person does not utter falsehoods.

As before, they had Dunwu tortured and interrogated further regarding the meal that had been provided for the bandits. This time, he implicated Kexiu. When Kexiu was dragged out, each one blamed the other. Kexiu's feet were pinioned together and flogged. He couldn't stand the pain, so he dodged the issue by confessing that as the abbot and head of the temple, I was solely responsible.

They summoned me again.

Before I went out, I told the assembled monks, "Once I answer this summons, you'll probably never see me again. All of you must be upright and mindful. Don't be frightened by what happens to me."

Just as before, I went out to answer the summons with a steady, unhurried stride. Joining my palms together, I bowed and stood before them.

Lord Chen demanded, "At your temple, you were feeding the bandits rice with winter melon for twelve days. I had a spy stationed among you who has ferreted out this information. Why are you concealing the truth?"

I saw that Kexiu's feet were being crushed in a vise with clamp sticks; Dunwu was tied up and kneeling next to him.

Shouting, I reprimanded both of them: "It's clear that over a hundred people spent twelve days at the temple and actually ate rice with winter melon. Why don't you admit it? You've put these three great lords to the trouble of interrogating you multiple times—and look at the suffering that you've brought upon yourselves!"

Smiling, the river surveillance magistrate said, "If you're really an honest person, why don't you tell me straightforwardly what happened?!"

I parried the question: "Does the Great Lord want to find out about our normal refectory operation and our customary temple fare over the years, or are you only looking into what we were eating on those twelve days?"

Lord Chen took the bait: "What's this about your normal diet through the years?"

I told him, "Mount Hua is the general name for all of the villages located within the range of a hundred *li* from the monastery. There are many monks living at the temple and many mouths to feed. Twice a year, during the summer and fall harvest seasons, the monks must go out to every village in order to muster supplies of wheat and millet. Thus, for our monastery, all of the surrounding villagers are almsgivers.

"Whenever a group of villagers comes to the temple, regardless of how many or how few visitors there are, we always hospitably offer them tea and rice. If they do not receive a cordial welcome when they visit us, we will not receive any grain donations the next year when we go on alms rounds. That has been our normal practice ever since the bronze pavilion was erected.

"Now, the food that was served on those twelve days during the eighth month was simply one instance of our customary procedure. The people who came to the temple on those days weren't carrying bows and arrows or any other weapons. How could we possibly judge whether or not they were bandits?"

The river controller conferred with Lord Ba and Lord Ao in Manchurian.

The interpreter translated for me: "The three great lords say that you are a frank, straightforward person. Your words are neither empty nor deceitful. The refectory issue requires no further investigation. You are dismissed!"

Walking at a steady pace, maintaining an impassive countenance

The above-mentioned magistrates also interrogated Dunwu on the temple's property and finances. Fearing torture, he told them everything about the monastery's landed property, its mountain fields, and so on. He reported every last detail to the officers, and then deflected their attention onto someone else. Money and the contents of the storehouse are under the jurisdiction of Fohui, he told the interrogators. They'd have to question Fohui for information on those matters.

Fohui was summoned for interrogation. He told the magistrates that there were thirty-six silver taels and eight or nine thousand mace in the business office coffers. This seemed like such a paltry sum that the magistrates angrily refused to believe him. They had Fohui tied up and flogged. He was unable to answer their questions and could only tell them that the abbot knew everything.

The district magistrate descended the slope and went to summon me. The lords Ba and Ao, who had seen me summoned multiple times, noted that I always walked into their presence with a steady pace and maintained an unflustered countenance.

They spoke to the interpreter, who translated for me: "The great lords are telling you to sit down. You have nothing to fear!"

The third summons

River Controller Chen outlined the dubious testimony: "The Mount Baohua temple is quite large and has many monks: it must take a considerable amount of money to run such an establishment. Why did the business office clerk tell us that the treasury only contains thirty-six silver taels?"

I answered, "The monastery clerk is afraid, so he couldn't give you a clear answer."

Chen pursued, "Well, how much money does the temple actually have?"

I replied, "My ordination and Dharma-transmission master, the Monk Sanmei, had extensive karmic connections. Many members of the nobility and government officials took refuge with him, so the temple was amply supplied with silver taels.

"Sanmei was large-hearted and gave money away freely. He never saved a cent; everywhere he went, he would have temples built and repaired, and would commission artisans to make Buddha images. In the last year of his life, he spent every last tael renovating Baohua Temple.

"Last year, during the intercalary sixth month, he passed away. Those of us who are his disciples do not have our master's expansive disposition and easygoing good fortune: our karmic foundation is feeble and constrained. There are many people in our monastic assembly, but our supplies are inadequate to support us.

"The temple used to have a black horse, but we had to sell it to a carriage-driver at the Nanjing Weaving Bureau for fifty-eight silver taels. In the last eight or nine days, we've already spent twenty-two taels, leaving us with only thirty-six taels remaining in our treasury. Great lords, if you don't believe me, just send someone to Nanjing to ask the carriage-driver. You'll find out for sure about our finances!"

The Rambling Story of a Dream

The three lords Ba, Ao, and Chen talked the matter over together. Finally, each of them nodded.

The interpreter told me, "The three grand lords say that you haven't lied to them. There's no need to send someone out to interrogate the carriage-driver."

At that, they had the ropes binding Fohui loosened. Afterwards, they summoned Xuanwen and Jixuan.

The river controller said, "It is my understanding that before being ordained at Baohua Temple, you two monks and Kexiu were originally local villagers. You are Mount Hua residents. Tie them up!"[404]

Addressing me, the river controller said, "The doings of these four people[405] do not concern you. You are dismissed!"

Not daring to look back at the sorry scene, I descended[406] and went back to sit with the other monks.[407]

Black bannermen are replaced by a squad of green bannermen.

By noon, the sun was scorching down on us; there were no trees to provide shade. We had been sitting there for quite a long time and everyone was famished; moreover, we were drenched in sweat, tormented by the oppressive heat.

All of a sudden, a black cloud sailed over us and covered the

---

404. Rebel bandits were mainly local peasants; hence, the Qing army was especially suspicious of common people and treated them with great severity.

405. No precise indication of the identity of these four people is given in the text. At this point, five people (besides Jianyue) have been summoned.

406. The military proceedings may have taken place on the mountain peak, with prisoners held lower down the slope.

407. The four monks had deflected blame for their shortcomings onto the abbot. Due to Jianyue's adroit responses, the generals, whose intention was to have them all executed, gave them the benefit of the doubt and let them go.

Those who keep the precepts do not use weapons

mountain peak like an enormous parasol. Light rays still shot out around its four edges, but it mercifully blocked out the overhead sunlight. Gradually, the shadows lengthened, and it was evening.

A soldier wielding a flag came up to us and hollered, "You elders, follow me."

I assumed that we were going out to our deaths; the monks' faces paled with apprehension. But much to our surprise, it turned out that some benevolent soldiers were stationed at the military camp.

The soldier joined his palms happily and told us, "Masters, you are saved! You were originally being held by the Black Banner[408] forces and would surely have been executed. The black bannermen have just been replaced by the Green Banner,[409] so you have nothing to fear. Take it easy!"

Looking up, I saw that the flag was indeed green. We were all unspeakably relieved.

Those who keep the precepts do not use weapons. We endure hunger together, and when food is available, we share it equally amongst ourselves.

The soldier carrying the flag led us to the foot of the mountain slope, where we sat down. Dozens of soldiers surrounded us and observed us sympathetically.

One of them declared, "Today, if this abbot hadn't come out several times to explain matters for you, you'd certainly never have gotten out alive. Sirs, you three[410] have been lucky."

---

408. Qing military units were eventually named for the banners they carried.

409. The Green Bannermen were all ethnic Han Chinese, whereas the original banner troops were primarily Manchurian or Mongolian.

410. The text does not identify Jianyue's companions in misery, nor are the many remaining Baohua monks accounted for.

Another soldier walked up to me and said, "You've had a grueling day—relax! Now, you can breathe freely."

At that, he unbuckled from his waist the bag in which he kept his bow and offered it to me as a pillow.

I said, "That's a deadly weapon: those who keep the precepts never use such things."

Another Han soldier addressed me: "You must be famished!"

He took a dry biscuit out of his satchel and presented it to me. I received the biscuit and broke it into small pieces so that everyone could have some.

He protested, "That's for you, there's no need to share it!"

I told him, "We live communally and conduct our spiritual practice together. We endure hunger together; when food is available, we share it equally among ourselves. Now, in such a miserable situation, how could I possibly not share this food!"

This elicited the admiration of the soldiers guarding us.

They had a discussion, and then said, "We are going to the village up ahead to do some cooking. Tomorrow morning, we'll bring you some food."

By midnight, we were unendurably thirsty. We noticed a small pond at the foot of the slope and ran down to it. When we drank its water, it tasted sweet and cool. At dawn, we could see it clearly: actually, it was a filthy pool that had been hollowed out by wallowing cattle.

The assembly elects me as their abbot. Confiscated temple property is restored. Three Qing officials become Dharma protectors.

At sunrise, a soldier came and led us out to the military tents.

Lord Chen, the river controller, told me, "You are a true

spiritual practitioner. We authorize you to act as the abbot of Baohua Temple. Lead your monks back to the monastery."

I told him, "At the present time, I won't be living at the monastery."

The river controller addressed the group: "Since he isn't a temple resident, you must elect a virtuous person from within your ranks who is capable of directing the monastery."

The assembly of monks spoke up in unison: "Only this abbot is suitable to act as our leader. No one else is qualified."

Lord Chen was amused: "I say that you're the abbot, and these monks have elected you, too. Why is it that you used to be the abbot, but now, you aren't?"

I replied, "The only reason I formerly acted as the abbot was that, when our late master passed away, his stūpa was still under construction. If I had abandoned it during a bandit uprising, everyone would blame me for unfilial conduct. That's why I didn't leave the monastery.

"Now, I've decided not to live there because over a hundred monks have been unjustly arrested. Fortunately, you three grand lords are clear-sighted and spared them from seemingly inevitable execution. We have been reborn from death.

"But even though we have been absolved from blame, Mount Hua is still a chronically disaster-prone area. If rebel bandits cross the mountain as before, some people will be sure to report that we're harboring criminals, and the saṃgha will be brought right back here to await execution. That's why I don't want to continue as the abbot. Even though the master's stūpa is still unfinished, at least I won't be found lacking in filial piety."

The lord river controller said, "There's no need to refuse this position so strenuously just because you have misgiv-

The Rambling Story of a Dream

ings about what might happen in the future. Ba, Ao, and I will all act as Dharma protectors. Thus, the incense and candles of Baohua will burn under the auspices of the Qing dynasty, and no soldiers will ever come to disturb you.

"From now on, if soldiers or anyone else invades the temple, you need only send us a note reporting the incident. I'll have them caught straightaway and beheaded. Tomorrow, I'll give you an official placard. Take it back to the temple with you and mount it in a conspicuous location."

At that, I replied, "In that case, I shall follow your orders and go back to live in the monastery. But one more issue must be brought to your attention. Imperial Eunuch Sun has reported that the temple's fields, mountain farmland, and other permanent temple property have been confiscated by government officials. They are not Sun's personal possessions. I beg that you have these properties restored to the temple."

Pleased to grant another request, the river controller had everything returned to the temple. I led the assembly in conveying our thanks, after which we went back to the monastery.

Way-follower Chen and Master Xiang

When we finally entered the great hall and worshipped the Buddha, the trauma of that harrowing ordeal suddenly overwhelmed us. We fell prostrate on the floor; our tears flowed uncontrollably. Some unimaginable chain of cause and effect had brought us back from the brink of the grave and led us here, so that we could look reverently up at the Buddha's golden visage!

A devotee living at the base of the mountain in Yanxiang Village had not forgotten us. Way-follower Chen, a disciple who had taken refuge, heard that on the thirteenth day of the month, Qing troops had come and surrounded the temple by night. Learning that all of the monks had been arrested and taken to the military camp, he was deeply distressed. On the fifteenth day, he wanted to ascend the mountain and find out what had happened, but his son and nephew objected.

"Right now," they remonstrated, "Qing troops are still camped on Mount Dongxie. Corpses are strewn all over the mountains and plains, and there are no travelers out on the roads. It's too soon to venture out there!"

He replied, "When a disciple learns that his master is in peril, how can he just stand aside and watch?!"

He set off at once. At midday, he arrived at the temple, only to find that the monks had already come back. When he asked us what had happened, I recounted everything that had transpired. Happy and greatly relieved, he went back home.

During the military takeover, Ācārya Xiangxue was at the Shangfang Temple in Zhenjiang conducting a retreat. The Dharma brothers Chun and Zhi had gone to Zhenjiang to purchase incense and candles. They rushed to the Shangfang Temple to seek lodging and met Master Xiang.

Master Xiang received them frostily: "There's been trouble at Mount Hua. If I put you up here, my retreat site will be implicated. Find someplace else to stay!"

Chun and Zhi went off with tears in their eyes. When they came back to the temple on the eighteenth day of the month, they told us all about it. Hearing their story, we sighed deeply.

I observed, "Mount Baohua is the site where our deceased elder's full-body stūpa lies. Master Xiang knows that we've been in danger, and yet feels not the slightest concern; moreover, he doesn't even bother to find out what's happened. When he meets survivors, he treats them coldly and callously, and sends them away!

"What's going on with our Master Xiang? How can it be that one of our own order treats us dismissively, while Way-follower Chen, a householder, demonstrates such profound friendship towards us?!"

Interrogating a traitor

Half a month later, a brawny fellow came to the temple. Judging by his clothing, he might have been a soldier from the military camp. By now, we monks were like birds who take fright at the merest twang of a bowstring: his appearance put us in a state of deep apprehension. I went forth to meet him and greeted him politely.

He told me, "The grand lord river controller has sent me here to procure a horse."

I returned, "The temple does indeed have a fine horse. You can ride it back!"

My words delighted him. I continued, "You can certainly have this horse, but you must first show us the proper credentials."

He took out a small note from his waist garments and handed it to me. I saw that the front of the letter was signed with red earth rather than imperial vermillion ink.

I took it and rebuked him sharply, "What gang of bandits do you belong to?! You have some gall trying to trick us into handing over our horse! Haven't you heard that the three grand lords Ba, Ao, and Chen are Mount Hua's Dharma protectors?

I ordered the temple wardens, "Lock this man up and

send him to the magistrates!"

He immediately dropped down heavily to a kneeling position, banging his head on the ground and begging for mercy.

"I didn't want to do this," he declared, "It was our chief Zhang Kun who ordered me to come here!"

He burst into tears and couldn't stop crying. Suddenly, it started to rain profusely, and he got soaking wet. All in all, the captive was in a pitiable state.

I told him, "Today, I'll let you go free. If this happens again, we won't spare you! Here, take these straw sandals and umbrella. Now, get out of here!"

He took off his leather boots and exchanged them for the straw sandals. Braving the downpour, he raced off. After that incident, Baohua was peaceful; the rebel bandits never troubled us again.

A lapse of temple discipline. We start building a wooden ordination platform for transmitting the complete precepts.

Midway in the second month of the sixth Shunzhi regnal year,[411] I acted as the catechist for a few of Dazhao's disciples. Their attitude towards monastic regulations was deliberately derisive and contemptuous. To make matters worse, when Master Da found out about their behavior, he took an indulgent attitude and never bothered to reprimand them.

Seeing their breezy disregard for Buddhist standards, I immediately descended the mountain and crossed the Yangtze River, intending to go to northern Wutai.[412] En

---

411. 1649, when Jianyue was 48 years old
412. This is the third time that Jianyue leaves Baohua.

The Rambling Story of a Dream

route, I reached a temple in Chuzhou's[413] Guanshan Village. There, I met Master Zhanyi, the business office manager, who invited me to stay at the temple and begged me to impart the precepts.

Back at Baohua, the senior monk Yuanyun set about rectifying the situation. Yuanyun was a staunch disciple of Sanmei, who was his tonsure master and ordination master; I had been Yuanyun's catechist. At the time when Master Da's disciples were creating discord, Yuanyun happened to be at Baohua studying the Vinaya. He came forward to address the situation, summoning everyone to the hall that had been dedicated to Sanmei. There, he lectured on the precepts and gave the temple residents and adherents a good scolding.

To Master Dazhao, he said, "The monk Jian was personally entrusted by the former master with the responsibility of succeeding him as abbot. This formerly decrepit monastery was given a new lease on life by Sanmei. As monks, it is only suitable that all of you scrupulously observe the Buddhist precepts and regulations and heed the Buddhist teachings. Your spiritual practice should be built upon the foundation of discipline.

"So, why do you annoy your present abbot by defiantly refusing to obey the monastic rules? Why are you destroying your own lineage?! By offending your current abbot, you are also offending the previous abbot!"

With his own hand, Yuanyun composed a public notice announcing that the ordinands had been expelled for grave violations of the Buddhist precepts. He then had the unruly disciples banished from the monastery. Master Dazhao

---

413. Chuzhou is a district in Anhui province.

arranged to go to Guanshan Village in Chuzhou with Liyan and Dade[414] to escort me back to Baohua.

Once again, the precepts and regulations were strictly enforced. We began the construction of a wooden ordination platform to be used for transmitting the full monastic precepts.[415] Over three thousand people came to us begging for ordination. The temple's grain stores were only sufficient to feed that vast crowd of ordinands for a few days. Despite this difficulty, meals continued to be served throughout the ordination period.[416]

A longevity retreat assembly

In winter of the sixth year of the Shunzhi regnal era, the leader of the Ning'guo prefecture longevity assembly came to me personally with an invitation to attend the event. I accepted his invitation and told him that we would work out the details closer to the starting date.

The seventh year of Shunzhi marked my fiftieth birthday.[417] Patrons and almsgivers bringing unsolicited donations came from the four directions. Distinguished, virtuous, venerable senior monks from every shrine and temple came to Baohua in a spirit of mutual loving-kindness and deference.

---

414. 'Transcending speech' and 'Great virtue'

415. According to Zhou Zhenru, Sanmei originally constructed a wooden ordination platform. In 1647, Jianyue had a new wooden platform built. In 1663, Jianyue had the old ordination platform dismantled and rebuilt in white marble.

Zhou Zhenru, "Transcending History: (Re)Building Longchang Monastery of Mount Baohua in the Seventeenth Century" (Religions 13, no. 4: 285, 2022, https://doi.org/10.3390/rel13040285).

416. Hongyi ruefully observes that none of the people in attendance altruistically volunteered to fast during the retreat.

417. Ven. Hongyi deduces that Jianyue was actually 49 years old at this time.

The Rambling Story of a Dream

One of the visitors was Master Mixin, who had been tonsured by Sanmei and had acted as one of the reverend witnesses at my full ordination. His intention was to usurp the position of abbot.

On the morning of the fifteenth day of the fourth month, I struck a board to convene the monastic assembly in the abbot's hall. Master Mi was also invited to attend the gathering.

I told the monks, "Since ancient times, monasteries have always respectfully invited people of exceptional virtue to act as abbots. Your humble servant is ill-equipped for this role and discouragingly lacking in merit. I will now place Master Mi in charge of keeping an accurate record of the net quantities of monies and grains that are received and disbursed by the monastery. At the moment, our storehouse holds over three hundred piculs[418] of rice, over two hundred silver taels, and exactly ninety thousand mace."

I withdrew 52,000 mace from the warehouse and distributed the sum equally amongst everyone in the assembly. Our supply of oil, salt, fresh and dried fruits and nuts, and so on, was sufficient to last for a year. Once I had turned over the responsibility to Master Mi, I took up residence in the east building. After that, I never again concerned myself with the monastery's internal affairs.

The next day was the sixteenth. With the saṃgha, I made preliminary arrangements for the retreat. On the seventeenth, I made an offering of incense at Sanmei's stupa and worshipped there. Afterwards, I formally took my leave.

The Vinaya stipulates that if interpersonal conflicts arise at a monastery, a person involved may attend a retreat held at another location.

---

418. A *picul* (or *dan*) is the amount that can be carried on a shoulder pole.

A longevity retreat assembly

Thus, I announced to the assembly, "Tomorrow morning, I'll be departing to attend a longevity retreat in Ning'guo prefecture."

After my announcement, everyone in the saṃgha came to me requesting permission to accompany me when I left the mountain.

I told them, "Our deceased master changed the orientation of Baohua Temple and caused it to rise to prominence once again; moreover, this is the site where our previous master entered nirvāṇa and where his relics are housed. For us, as members of the Vinaya lineage, it is our ancestral hermitage. Originally, my intention was to devote my life to cleaning and sweeping our master's shrine, but circumstances have prevented me from fulfilling my vow.

"Now, let's deal with both issues, so that our master's shrine is honored, and you can still attend the Ning'guo retreat with me. If you are willing to take my place as an attendant at our ancestral hermitage and are resolved to practice extreme asceticism, please stand on my left. You can always go to the retreat later. Those who are resolved to descend the mountain with me, stand on my right side."

Once I had delineated the two choices, they sorted themselves into groups. Those who wanted to accompany me to the retreat comprised well over a half—as I recall, over a hundred people wanted to go.

At dawn on the eighteenth day, Lüzhong, the assistant business office manager, gave the group that was accompanying me thirty silver taels to cover our travel expenses. Smiling, I refused the money.

He protested, "But, this is alms money that was especially donated to you—it was never intended for the monks here."

The Rambling Story of a Dream

"They donated the money to one of us, which is tantamount to giving it to all of us!" I replied.

After breakfasting, we set off down the mountain.[419] When we got to Laopeng Bridge, we encountered Wayfollower Zhang, who invited us to a vegetarian meal and then hired a boat for us. That evening, we lodged at the Erzhong ancestral temple in Xiaguan.

The Erzhong business office manager was one of my ordinand disciples. He cordially hosted us for three days, during which time, quite a few virtuous believers came to take refuge. Those pious visitors presented us with over forty piculs of rice and a total of one hundred silver taels.

We then hired a boat and sailed upstream, finally reaching Ning'guo at the close of the fourth month. At the assembly, our host treated us with great cordiality. He and I were on excellent terms.

My residence on the mountain inspires the local people.

Early in the fifth month, a few of the disciples who had stayed behind at Baohua came to join us. Their news was that after I had descended the mountain, an elder from Jurong county found out about Master Mixin's campaign to assume the role of abbot, my conceding the position to him, and my subsequent departure. He immediately had Mixin summoned to the Longtan Temple in Xiayuan Village, where he reprimanded the usurper soundly and gave him half a month to go after me and bring me back to Baohua.

---

419. This is the fourth time that Jianyue leaves Baohua.

Inspiring the local people

Afterwards, Dharma protector Chen Minzhao[420] came to the mountain to worship the Buddha. Upon hearing that I was no longer there, he cried so bitterly that he went hoarse.

Finally, he told the monks, "Now that Baohua's Monk has departed, this monastery is abandoned and defeated. The root of this calamity does not lie exclusively with Mixin; it was instigated by the entire body of temple adherents. It would be perfectly appropriate to have everyone hauled off to the magistrate and severely punished.

"For the time being, you will be spared: as a Dharma protector, my priority is to protect and sustain the saṃgha, which is one of the three Buddhist treasures. An appropriate date will be set for me to go to Xuancheng[421] personally and escort the Monk back to Baohua."

On the twenty-first day of the seventh month, Dharma Protector Chen arrived in Xuancheng, where he met me, brought me up to date on his recent trip to Baohua, and explained the reason for his current visit.

I felt ashamed: my heart was deeply moved by his sincere intention to protect and uphold the Dharma. Hence, on the twenty-fourth day, I ordered the group of monks who had accompanied me to take a boat back to Baohua, while I took an overland route with Dharma Protector Chen. We reached Jiang'ning on the twenty-ninth.

The next day, the monk Juelang, Chen Minzhao, and the other Dharma protectors escorted me back to the Mount Hua area. Towards nightfall, we passed through

---

420. Ven. Hongyi found relevant written communications from Chen Minzhao in the late-Ming work *Lingfeng zong lun* written by the Buddhist scholar-monk Ouyi Zhixu (1599–1655).

421. A city in southeast Anhui province. Ning'guo is a county-level city under the administration of Xuancheng.

Fanjiachang. When the local villagers heard that I was returning to Baohua, men and women competed to get a glimpse of the procession, while others lit the way for us with flaming brands that illuminated our path as brightly as if it were broad daylight.

Laughing loudly, Juelang said, "What a spectacle!!"

Then, he commented to the Dharma protectors, "Just see how people are moved and inspired when Master Jian is in residence on the mountain! It is an auspicious omen: truly, the Way will flourish!"

Back at Baohua, I rectify lax management and strengthen monastic discipline.

The next day, I summoned the department officials who remained at the monastery to a meeting. Our goal was to plan a vegetarian banquet for our Dharma protectors in recognition of their faithful support.

When asked what temple property we still possessed, the temple superintendent[422] Ruojian answered, "We have neither silver taels nor mace, and there are only a few piculs of rice left in our warehouse. Our storehouses are empty."

I sighed, "I've been gone for less than five months—how can things have gotten into such a state?"

"After you left, Monk," Ruojian returned, "the temple no longer seemed like a Vinaya hall. Everyone who remained here just did as they pleased. Every day, Master Mi regaled himself with lavish meals. Since we never had any income, our supplies were quickly exhausted. It was just like drawing water from a stagnant pool: since the pool isn't fed by a living

---

422. *jianyuan*

Stricter monastic discipline

spring, its waters are quickly depleted. That's what happened to us; I didn't have the authority to turn things around."

Hearing this, the Dharma protectors scowled, greatly displeased.

Trying to smooth things over, I declared, "The circumstances governing my previous exit from and return to Baohua are unlike those that have determined my present retreat and return: in the first case, we were incarcerated, while in the second case, I was replaced by another abbot. The karmic situations are different, so we needn't get unduly aggravated, as though this were a recurrent problem. Just take things as they come!"

As time went by, more and more people came to the monastery from near and far asking to receive the precepts.

I cautioned these visitors about what they were letting themselves in for: "On Mount Baohua, our lives are plain, poor, and honest. If we host extra people at meals, we can only provide them with additional dippers of water; we cannot refill our guests' rice bowls. If you can't cope with such harsh living conditions, you'd better go to another temple."

Despite my warning, everyone willingly stayed on the mountain; no one left to find a more comfortable location.

Starting from the beginning of the eighth Shunzhi regnal year, during the winter and summer semesters, our assembly would gather in one hall along with monastics from other hermitages. For seven days and nights, the group would recite the Buddha's name continuously. At noon, we had a single meal of porridge; no food was taken in the afternoon. These regulations were observed consistently, without alteration.

On the fifteenth day of the seventh month, a repentance ceremony was held to mark the close of the summer retreat.

The Rambling Story of a Dream

Afterwards, we celebrated the *Ullambana* festival,[423] as set forth in the *Ullambana Sūtra*. Every bit of money and other property owned by the abbot was distributed amongst the participants to repay profound parental blessings. At Baohua, this became an established practice.

We reduce temple rations in order to feed our starving neighbors. Supplicants chant the Buddha's name and cultivate blessings.

During the ninth Shunzhi regnal year,[424] the Jiang'nan region was afflicted by swarms of locusts and acute drought. Not an inch of grass grew, and the common folk were starving. The villagers—both old and young, male and female alike—came up the mountain begging for food. Not all of these people were beggars, some were landowners. In all, one or two hundred needy people came to us.

I told the saṃgha, "We'll cut back on our individual grain rations so that we can relieve the people's suffering."

At noon one day, we had several times more visitors than ever before; the temple buildings and cloisters were mobbed with people. I took this as an opportune moment to demonstrate and elucidate the Buddhist teachings.

"Today, you have come here as a last resort. Consider the chain of causation that has brought you to this moment. In previous lifetimes, you did not believe in the three treasures of Buddhism. You were greedy, stingy, and unwilling to make charitable donations to aid the poor and needy. You

---

423. An observance in which offerings are made to feed the legions of hungry ghosts. Also known as Saṃgha Day, it honors the Buddhist saṃgha that has successfully completed an entire rains retreat.

424. Ven. Jianyue was now 51 years old.

are now experiencing the fruits of your previous actions.

"I am now proposing a plan to the monks here: Let's donate three cash pennies to everyone who has come here today."

Then, I told the supplicants, "Once you have received your pennies, I will go to each of you and let you donate one cash penny back to me. You will offer your donation with both hands uplifted while reciting the Buddha's name.

"By doing this, I am helping each of you to gain merit by making an offering to the Saṃgha Treasure. In this way, you will begin to cultivate purity and establish a personal field of blessings. As time goes on, this meritorious seed will develop, and you will be released from poverty."

For an instant while I promulgated the Dharma, the Buddha's voice roared like thunder.

Afterwards, I commanded the monks to clear out the contents of our warehouse. Every grain of rice that we had in storage was cooked and served. Once the supplicants had eaten their fill, they chanted the Buddha's name and went on their way.

After we had distributed our stored rice, the temple's grain supply was insufficient to last overnight. The next morning, we boiled a pot of water in place of our morning meal. To our astonishment, a lay Buddhist from Jiang'ning named Huang Junfu arrived that evening with a donation of ten piculs of rice!

Visiting bhikṣuṇīs do not bow to the male saṃgha. I compile a guide entitled "Admonishing Bhikṣuṇīs on Proper Deportment and Discipline."

Xinwen, a fifty-year-old nun from Hanyang prefecture

The Rambling Story of a Dream

in the Chu region,[425] made a vow to uphold the precepts. Leading nine disciples, she took a boat to Mount Baohua, undeterred by the enormous distance and hazardous travel conditions. In the middle of the second month of the tenth year of Shunzhi,[426] the ten nuns arrived at the temple and begged to do a three-month retreat with us. They brought us a donation of sixty piculs of rice and twenty silver taels. Noting their sincerity and earnest, forthright speech, I felt compassion and sympathy for them and approved their retreat.

One day, she sponsored a vegetarian meal for the saṃgha, but was unwilling to enter the dining hall and make her obeisance to the monks. Once the meal was over, I summoned her to appear before the monastic assembly.

"You have come from afar with the firm intention of learning the precepts," I told her, "Why didn't you enter the refectory and bow to the monks? Buddhist regulations stipulate that even a bhikṣuṇī who has been ordained for a hundred years must bow to a newly-ordained monk. Today, you bhikṣuṇīs have demonstrated pride and arrogance by showing disrespect to monks. You are certainly not genuine students of the precepts!"

She countered, "Your humble servant is from the Chu region. Whenever I find out about places where there are virtuous friends, I always pay them a visit and treat them to a vegetarian banquet. The abbots in our locality reciprocate by treating me with great hospitality. No one has ever expected me to bow."

---

425. Chu was an ancient kingdom that was defeated by the Qin. The Chu region comprised modern Hubei and Hunan provinces, as well as some areas in Guizhou, Chongqing, Henan, Anhui, Jiangxi, Jiangsu, Zhejiang, and Shanghai.

426. when Jianyue was 52 years old

A guide for bhikṣuṇīs

I corrected her sharply: "Such people covet material gain and undermine the Dharma Gate. When they see a bhikṣuṇī who is willing to support them, they pander to her and treat her like their own mother, hoping to obtain lavish donations. Such people are like bugs in a lion's fur—they are certainly not virtuous friends. Currently, Mount Baohua is poor, but upright. We would rather endure hunger than violate the Buddhist precepts and regulations by courting favor with affluent donors.

"To rectify this error, we will consider today's banquet to have been hosted by our own residents. The silver taels that were used to purchase food will be refunded to you in full. The rice that you brought will be placed in the lower courtyard. Take it with you. Now, go somewhere else!"

Puzzled by my outburst, the senior nun received the money and led her disciples down via the back side of the mountain. That night, they lodged at the Chushuidong hermitage. As this was happening, a disciple named Gutan came to the abbot's quarters to intercede on the nuns' behalf.

"Please consider the situation from a broader perspective," he urged. "Those nuns have come from a distant place to visit us. As it happens, our storehouse is empty. Monk, please utilize skillful means and accept the nuns' gifts. By treating them with flexibility, you will affirm and reinforce their Way-mind; moreover, you will provide this assembly with half a month of sustenance."

I fixed him with a stern gaze. "As long as our spiritual practice is true," I thundered, "the saṃgha will never suffer hunger. In our present honest but impoverished circumstances, we can establish the Dharma Gate by means of upright speech and action, even though we have no tangible offerings to make. How can a Vinaya master who upholds the precepts violate the divine regulations by stooping to gain mundane profits?!"

Gutan's face reddened. He bowed and withdrew from the room.

Three days later, Xinwen Bhikṣuṇī and her disciples came back up the mountain.

Weeping, they knelt outside the abbot's door and said, "We never understood the precepts when we were in the Chu region; hence, this regrettable misunderstanding has occurred. We were certainly not showing pride and arrogance; we had no intention of treating the monks rudely! We implore you, Monk, to show compassion and deign to hear our repentance. Hereafter, we will comply with all of your teachings!"

The heads of every temple department supported the nuns' entreaty. In the end, the nuns went to Lushan Village, where they established a territory for their retreat. As is stipulated in the Vinaya, ācāryas and other masters from Baohua were sent to admonish and preach to the nuns every half month. At these times, our monks gave the nuns explanatory sermons based on the text *The Original Vinaya*.[427]

Due to this incident, I resolved to produce a compendium entitled "Admonishing Bhikṣuṇīs on Proper Deportment and Discipline,"[428] to be circulated amongst Buddhist communities.

---

427. *Benbu pini*
428. *Jiaojie biqiuni zheng' fan*

The Pratyutpanna-samādhi retreat

I undergo a three-month-long pratyutpanna-samādhi retreat twice.[429]

In the early days of the eighth lunar month, Huiyi, the rear hall monk, was browsing through the Chinese Buddhist canon. He was originally from the Chu region and had spent a long time learning and practising tenets of the Chan tradition. When he came to Baohua, he took refuge with me and began studying the Vinaya.

One day, the temple's scriptures were taken out for an airing in the sunshine. Huiyi noticed the *Pratyutpanna-samādhi sūtra*[430] and was moved to read it.

The next day, he told me, "This *Panzhou sanmei sūtra* is an important teaching of the Jingye[431] tradition. It is by far the most difficult teaching to practise."

I affirmed his judgement: "When I was in northern Wutai, a virtuous friend instructed me on the *Panzhou sanmei* scripture. He told me that those who practise its teachings must remain standing for ninety days straight without sitting or lying down.

"When I got to this temple, I perused the *Collected Biographical Works Concerning the Nanshan Vinaya Patriarch Daoxuan*[432] and discovered that Patriarch Xuan had frequently practised this meditation method. After Daoxuan's time, however, fewer and fewer spiritual aspirants attempted it.

---

429. a type of *samādhi* in which the buddhas of the ten directions are seen as clearly as stars in the night sky

430. *Meditation in which the buddhas of the present stand before the practitioner: Panzhou sanmei jing* [Ch]

431. Master Daoxuan (596–667) is the patriarch of the *Dharmaguptaka* Vinaya lineage. He died at the Jingye Temple of Shaanxi province, where his *stūpa* stands.

432. *Nanshan Daoxuan lüzu xingji*

Those who are capable of total renunciation will naturally achieve this type of samādhi."

Motivated by our discussion, I selected the twentieth day of the eighth month as the starting date for my retreat. For ninety days straight, I planned to stay in the abbot's quarters and emulate the worthies of the past. Vowing to follow in the Vinaya Patriarch's footsteps, I cut myself off from all outside affairs and entered a three-month retreat. I emerged from the retreat on the twenty-first day of the eleventh month.

In the autumn of the twelfth Shunzhi regnal year,[433] I again underwent a ninety-day standing retreat. Thus, I enjoyed the immeasurable good fortune of planting the seeds of purity twice. Nevertheless, I still felt deep shame over the heavy impediments that continued to block my path to liberation. During those two retreats, I never realized the crowning spiritual benefits that had been achieved by past adepts.

I compose a Vinaya compendium as a guide for countless future generations of aspirants.

To promote the accurate practice of the Vinaya, I have corrected previously-condoned expedient measures that deviated from Buddhist regulations. Thus, I now uphold the Dharma with utmost strictness and fidelity. I have composed a guidebook entitled *The Definitive Vinaya*[434] for those seeking to identify erroneous practices and transmit the proper Buddhist tradition. I have supported instruction and training; to that end, I've had

---

433. when Jianyue was 54 years old
434. *Pini zhengfan*

Fortifying the Buddha-gate

an ordination platform built for the transmission of the precepts. These projects and others will serve as models for posterity.

I have purchased mountain fields to provide for the monastic assembly. Our venerable abbot had the temple's orientation changed, but some of his objectives remained unrealized during his lifetime. Thus, every small or large-scale construction project that I have carried out is intended to fulfill his long-term vision for Baohua.

For decades, I have worked painstakingly. My intention has always been to brace up the Buddha-gate with an iron spine and promulgate the Dharma. I have accomplished all of these things in recognition of the former Monk's profound grace in bestowing upon me the milk of the Vinaya teachings.[435]

I have now related to you every last detail of my life, even though my narrative might seem cumbersome and tedious. The events that I have just related have been witnessed by Liyan Ācārya and all of the chief disciples who have been my attendants for many years.

But please bear in mind that all appearances are illusory. When I look back upon things that happened in the past, I know that they are only a dream. That is why this autobiography is entitled *The Rambling Story of a Dream*.

---

435. *śīla-dharma* [Skt]

To conclude, I will add this *gatha*:[436]

In a dream, my southward trek lasted for many autumns;
 Now, I can finally rest after that arduous journey.

 You've asked me today to recount my travels,
But I can only entertain you with scenes from a dream.

---

436. a poem, mantra, or funeral verse

Appendices

A Thumbnail History of Baohua Monastery

The monastery in the Baohua hills figures importantly in this autobiography and merits its own brief introduction. It was the only temple in this range of hills; hence, it was designated by the term *shan* (mountain). Lying around twenty miles northeast of Nanjing, it has long been renowned for its bronze pavilion flanked by beamless halls.

Although the ancient temple is called 'Baohua' (Precious Flower) or 'Hua' throughout Jianyue's narrative, it was given a succession of names during its existence. When the temple was first built during the Liang dynasty (502–557), it was simply known as Master Baojie's hermitage, so named for the Chan master who had taken up residence on the mountain. Later on in the sixth century, it was called the Qianhua (Thousand Flower) Temple. During the Ming dynasty, it was rechristened the Longchang (August Glory) Temple by the Wanli Emperor. During the Qing era, the main temple was renamed the Huiju (Abiding Wisdom) Temple by the Kangxi Emperor.

As marks of imperial favor, the monastery received precious volumes of Buddhist scriptures and funding for architectural projects. Esteeming Baohua's rigorous and comprehensive ordination training, Qing-dynasty emperors would schedule retreats at Baohua despite its austerity and relative poverty, passing over grander temples. At

Baohua, special quarters and domestic services were available for imperial guests.

The earliest recorded Buddhist presence on Baohua was Master Baojie (502–557), a Chan monk. Miaofeng Fudeng (1540–1612), a Chan monk who had temple-building experience and imperial sponsorship, constructed the Huiju monastery in 1605. Its lavish design featured a bronze pavilion with vaulted stone beamless halls on its right and left sides. Miaofeng never established a community on Baohua, nor did he or his successors assume the role of abbot. By the time of Jianyue's autobiography, the monastery had fallen into desuetude.

At that point, Sanmei Jiguang was asked to lead and renovate the foundering monastery. He had the temple's orientation changed, commissioned a ring of buildings around the temple's central courtyard, and erected an ordination platform. Jianyue, Sanmei's successor, constructed buildings around those that had been commissioned by his predecessor and built two additional gateways. His many contributions also included rebuilding stables, workshops where tea and tofu were produced, and a meditation hall. Jianyue rebuilt Sanmei's ordination platform twice—once in wood, and then in elaborately-carved white marble. When Ding'an took over the abbotship from Jianyue, he continued to build around the temple's central courtyard complex.

At the time of this narrative, Chan, Vinaya, and Pure Land traditions were practised at the monastery. Sanmei Jiguang had been trained in the Chan and Pure Land traditions before his ordination under the Vinaya master Guxin Ruxin. Sanmei's disciple Jianyue began to enforce the Vinaya code of discipline rigorously. Although his revisions were initially met with dismay and displeasure by many of the monastery's resident monks, Baohua's reputation as a model temple grew. From the Qing dynasty to the Republican era, it was regarded as China's preeminent Buddhist center.

Buddhist Temple Administrators

Buddhist temples were often enormous compounds comprised of a large monastic population, numerous buildings, spacious lands, and sizeable stores of furnishings and supplies. As in the imperial court, an administrative bureaucracy was in place to regulate the many facets of monastic life and keep the community supplied with its spiritual and material necessities. Although in theory, the monastic bureaucracy was systematically organized, actual temple administration was often modified.

Location, geography, political climate, and chronology engendered widely divergent administrative structures. Various temples and hermitages appear in the narrative, not all of which would have required the same set of personnel. Over time, the administrative staff at Baohua evolved from a skeleton crew after the Qing takeover to what can be inferred was a robust hierarchy by the time that Jianyue was respectfully asked to recount his memoirs. Thus, the official positions enumerated below are not necessarily applicable to all temples, nor do they apply to every phase of a monastery's history.

Large Buddhist monasteries were like miniature cities. A variety of skilled workers, such as tailors, builders, carpenters, and printers, lived and worked in the temple compound. Sometimes, laypersons performed menial tasks in the refectory or guest hall. Special quarters were set aside for different types of workers, who would usually sleep at or nearby their workplace.

Jobs were assigned according to the capacities of individual monks, who carried out their duties with varying degrees of integrity. As can be seen in this narrative, Jianyue was strong, energetic, and capable, so the abbot Sanmei entrusted him with numerous responsibilities. Jianyue's rigorous work ethic, however, was not necessarily replicated by his successors. As an abbot, Jianyue instituted strict limitations on his personal power and privileges, although as time went on and Baohua's reputation grew, its abbots reverted to enjoying luxuries like private chefs, personal stoves, stores of special delicacies to eat, and a "royal" court of attendants.[437]

Local geography influenced temple functions. For example, Baohua's monks all had to lend a hand when supplies were transported up the mountain. On the other hand, a monastery situated in a low-lying urban area would naturally enjoy more convenient supply lines. Geography aside, Baohua's pool of available labor was decimated during the bandit uprisings; hence, its few remaining residents had to chip in to keep the temple running, regardless of their monastic rank.

Idiosyncratic architectural design could also dictate the responsibilities of certain monks. Prip-Møller observes that in one temple, the monk in charge of boiling bath water also soaked salted vegetables, as the salting vats were located next to the bath house.[438]

---

437. Johannes Prip-Møller, *Chinese Buddhist Monasteries: Their Plan and Its Function as a Setting for Buddhist Monastic Life* [2d ed.]. (Hong Kong: Hong Kong University Press, 1967), 367.

438. *ibid.*, 359

The Rambling Story of a Dream

Along the route of Jianyue's pilgrimage, we sometimes see once-prominent temples that were in a state of decay, whereas the grand temple at Nanjing was amply populated with monastics and lay-persons. It can be assumed that the latter establishment would have enjoyed a full quota of administrators, which would not have been true for its dispirited brethren.

The information collected below is a rough attempt to describe the functions of temple officials that appear in the text, as well as some of the unnamed corps of workers who kept the castle-like establishment going. The peripatetic narrative takes place in a variety of Buddhist temples, making it difficult to pin down the local duties of each functionary with certainty.[439] The most nuanced information on monastic life can be found in the twentieth-century research of Holmes Hinkley Welch (1921–1981) and Johannes Prip-Møller (1889–1943), who were writing centuries after the time of Ven. Jianyue. Since monasteries are conservative entities, it can be inferred that the research of these eminent scholars also applies to Baohua's earlier circumstances.

In order to avoid ambiguity, it is tempting to avoid the issue of monastic bureaucracy altogether and only include pinyin transliterations of official positions in this translation. Given that the available Western equivalents for monastic titles are perforce drawn from military or ecclesiastic analogues, assigning titles reminiscent of British bureaucracy is at best only a *pis-aller*. For reference, additional information is supplied below and in the footnotes.

---

439. Holmes Welch aptly observes, "It is difficult to find English equivalents that fit the duties of each rank, which in some cases were purely ceremonial while in other cases there were no duties at all." Holmes Welch, *The Practice of Chinese Buddhism,* 1900–1950, (Cambridge: Harvard University Press, 1973), 61. https://terebess.hu/zen/mesterek/Holmes-Welch-The-Practice.pdf

Appendices

1. **Some monastic departments and compounds**
   - Business office: *kufang*
   - Guest department: *ketang*
   - Sacristy: *yiboliao*
   - Refectory: *daliao*
   - Grounds department: *wai zhishi*
   - Health clinic: *ruyi liao*
   - Novice hall: *xinjie tang*
   - Meditation hall: *chan tang*
   - Ordination platform: *jietan*

2. **The general term for any monastic administrative position is *zhishi* (official, officer).**

3. **The abbot and the four class leaders**
   - The head of a monastery was the **abbot** (*fangzhang heshang*). In the narrative, Sanmei is referred to as the Monk (*heshang*), a shortened version of this title.

   The abbot's four main assistants were the four hall leaders, who were chosen on the basis of prestige and seniority. These distinguished monks were entitled to stand in for the abbot when he was otherwise engaged and were charged with religious instruction and discipline. They lived in administrative quarters located on two sides of the Chan meditation hall. As senior monastics, they stood in the western row on ceremonial occasions.

- The **head seat** (*shouzuo, shangzuo, zhengzuo*: rector, presiding monk) was the front hall[440] class leader who supervised the group's moral behavior and spiritual practice. A model of proper monastic decorum, this monk led the assembly during meals, chanting, and meditation. Second only to the abbot, this monk was authorized to check on vegetarian meals in the kitchen and assign punishments for precept violations. The rector held the highest position in the abbot's cabinet and acted as his advisor. Only one monk served in this capacity.

- The **west hall** (*xitang*: senior instructor) was a monastic of lesser importance whose status was similar to that of any ordinary monastic seeking instruction. A person of proven virtue, his responsibilities included teaching and giving sermons. This instructor could also be a retired senior monk from another abbey. Three or four people could hold this position simultaneously.

- The **rear hall** (*houtang*: associate instructor) supported and encouraged the group seated on the rear platform of the meditation hall. Although this person had no specific ongoing jobs, he was available to carry out ad hoc assignments designated by the abbot, and could act as an advisor to the head seat. The rear hall was expected to oversee assemblies and ensure that rituals were in keeping with the temple's

---

440. 'Hall' (*tang*) signifies a group of ordinands or a class. In the translation, both 'group' and 'class' are substituted for 'hall.'

Appendices

designated Buddhist tradition; additionally, he oversaw disciplinary education. Three or four monastics could serve in this role.

- As the head of the meditation hall, the **hall chief** (*tangzhu*: assistant instructor) served as the novice master, a crucial temple responsibility. The hall head was a person of proven virtue with a sound spiritual practice. He was assigned to jobs not covered by the above group leaders (*banshou*). This officer was in charge of the meditation hall and the chanting hall. There was only one hall chief.

4. **Various monastic officers and menial workers**

    Whereas the previous group of administrators was in charge of the temple's spiritual practice, the following prefects ran the physical plant, dining facilities, storeroom, treasury, grounds, and guest dormitory. Several alternative English translations for these positions appear below. The information on their responsibilities is not always uniform, and the administrative duties associated with individual offices often seem to be overlapping and ambiguous.

    - The **superintendent**, **manager**, or **comptroller** (*jianyuan, jianzi*) was in charge of a wide range of business matters. This prefect managed the warehouse/business office (*kufang*), where daily necessities like comestibles and ritual implements were kept; he also acted as the accountant and property manager. He oversaw temple repairs, interacted with almsgivers, and kept yearly records. An extremely conscientious person was needed for this role. There was also an **assistant comptroller** (*fusi, fu jianyuan*).

- As a liaison between a monastery and the outside world, the **guest master** (*zhike, zhibin*) occupied a crucial position. Government dignitaries, almsgivers, and eminent monks from other temples were hospitably received by this officer, who would arrange for their tea and meals, schedule interviews with resident monastics, and assign dormitory space. This prefect examined each visiting monk's ordination certificate, verified its authenticity, and interrogated *yunshui* monks in order to root out those of questionable character. The guest master's duties might also include other sundry jobs like keeping the night watch, looking after candles and incense, or acting as a shrine attendant.

- The **provost, proctor, supervisor** (*sengzhi, jiucha*) served as a liaison between the abbot and the monastery. This officer led the daily worship services and oversaw monastic discipline and decorum. Throughout the day, he would observe and critique the monks' walking, standing, sitting, and lying down postures. He also admonished those who had lapsed, assigned penalties for transgressions, and judged the authenticity of government-issued ordination certificates. This officer was empowered to correct the abbot. As an overseer and inspector, he assisted the guest prefect and rector.

- The rector, **precentor** (*weina, karmadāna*) was a somewhat higher-ranking official than the

Appendices

provost. Besides managing the meditation hall, he might also oversee the refectory and temple buildings. This prefect also made announcements, struck gongs or boards in accordance with the daily schedule, supervised morning washing (the meditation compound had its own bathroom), appointed minor functionaries, and acted as the precentor during monastic offices. The rector advised the meditation monks, arranged group work, and determined punishments for precept violations. Because of the highly-regimented schedule that newly-ordained monks followed as meditation monks, the rector's job was crucial: the time spent in the meditation hall was required training for those who sought to obtain important administrative posts.

- The **refectory chief, chef** (*dianzuo*) oversaw meal preparation and dining facilities. His was a demanding, never-ending job that involved enforcing cleanliness and punctuality, avoiding waste, procuring fresh vegetables and kitchen staples, and supervising the entire cooking process. The chef worked with the warehouse manager and conferred with the comptroller and labor steward (*zhisui*). Classified among the high-level officers, the chef was not considered a menial laborer. A platoon of kitchen workers acted under the leadership of this monk.

- **Waiter** (*xingtang*): scullery duty

- The "cloud-water" **dormitory manager** (*liaoyuan, liaozhu*) supervised the living quarters that were assigned to itinerant monks, as well as the quarters assigned to important guests. "Cloud-water" (*yunshui*) monks were novices who traveled to various monasteries in order to train with capable teachers. The dormitory manager assigned seating in the meditation training hall (*gua dan*) and oversaw all of the monastery's guests. When extra help was needed for special banquets or labor parties, the dormitory manager was in charge of enlisting monks from the guest dormitory.

- The **supervisory clerk** (*kusi*) was in charge of village agents and kept track of the equipment that was loaned to the monastery's tenants.

- The abbot's entourage—literally, the "**robe and bowl**" (*yibo*)—was a corps of attendants who lived and worked in the abbot's quarters. The "Master of the Robe and the Bowl" (*yibo shi*) was the abbot's chief private valet. This monk was in charge of the storeroom where the head monk's ceremonial robes and alms bowl were housed. The abbot's attendants also oversaw the temple's money and treasured objects. Record-keeping and supervision of the grand abbot hall might also fall within the *yibo*'s jurisdiction.

- The **warehouse supervisor** (*kufang, fangtou*) had a wide range of duties. This person kept track of food, non-comestible goods, and Dharma equipment like candles and incense; he might also see to the upkeep of the monastery's fields, woods, lands, and temple buildings. Additionally, he might oversee the distribution of Dharma property (property of the Three Jewels), such as sūtras and scrolls. Although the term literally means 'storehouse,' *kufang* was used to indicate the business office.

- The (facilities/business office) **chief manager** (*dangjia seng, dangjia shi*; lit., "in charge of the house") had a private office in the business compound. This prefect met with outside business agents and was second to the abbot in status.

- **Central Buddhist Registry**: a government agency that monitored the population, certificates, and discipline of monastic communities. These government positions were held by reputable senior monks who came from monasteries in the capital city.

- The **labor steward** (*zhisui*) assigned tasks to novices and arranged communal labor. This steward was in charge of maintaining temple buildings and grounds. In Chinese, the title literally signifies a one-year duty, since the position was reassigned annually.

- The **secretary** (*shuji*) was in charge of written communication with government officials and almsgivers; he also made announcements that were posted in the temple or the outside community. This job required someone who was linguistically adroit and had elegant handwriting.

- The **prior** (*dusi*) had a comprehensive supervisory role in temple bureaucracy. Practical matters like finances, supplies, and government interactions lay within this officer's jurisdiction.

The Rambling Story of a Dream

- **Rice steward** (*fantou*)
- The **head of the novice class** preparing for ordination (*banshou*)
- **Verger**: the monk in charge of incense and lanterns (*xiangdeng*)
- **Department heads** (*fangtou*)
- **Cashier** (*siku*)
- **Attendance registrar**, secretary (*neiqin*)
- **Supervisory clerk** (*kutou*): a functionary who was charged with keeping track of the temple's day-to-day income and expenditure, its grains and monies. This monk stood in the east row. It was a crucial job, but of relatively low status.
- **Monastery director, prior** (*douguan, dousi*): This monk was in charge of practical affairs, such as finances, supplies, and diplomacy.

5. Ordination Trainers

- *yinli shi*: initiation masters
- *jiaoshou shi*: preceptor, catechist
- *jiemo shi*: karman instructor

East and West Rows

Note: This list is only intended to furnish a rough idea of what is meant when monastics are depicted as forming rows on either side of the abbot. Not all of these titles appear in the text, nor did the monasteries mentioned in the narrative necessarily have such personnel. Jianyue's autobiography deals with the vicissitudes of his own personal path, leaving such details to be visualized by his readers. The following information comes directly from *The Practice of Chinese Buddhism* by Holmes Welch.[441]

In imitation of the imperial practice of grouping courtiers into civil and military units and stationing them on either side of the emperor during formal assemblies, the four teaching leaders stood on the west side of the abbot,[442] while officials who dealt with the temple's practical affairs were stationed on the east side.

Welch divides temple personnel by rank and office, admitting that ambiguity existed between the two groups. He avers that a monastic's rank, their institutional status, might be relatively high, yet the job that they chose to do might be rather menial. Thus, 'office' designates a job.[443]

---

[441]. Holmes Welch, *The Practice of Chinese Buddhism*, 1900–1950, (Cambridge: Harvard University Press, 1973), 421–423. https://terebess.hu/zen/mesterek/Holmes-Welch-The-Practice.pdf

[442]. In theory, the main monastery gate faced south, as did the abbot during formal assemblies. Due to the exigencies of geography, however, the main gate's orientation was always defined as "south," regardless of its actual placement.

[443]. Holmes Welch, *The Practice of Chinese Buddhism*, 33–34.

The Rambling Story of a Dream

West Offices
Chef: *dianzuo*
Taster: *tie'an*
Rice steward: *fantou*
Vegetable steward: *caitou*
Water steward: *shuitou*
Stoker: *huotou*
Tea steward: *chatou*
Waiter: *xingtang*

Gatekeeper: *mentou*
Sanitation steward: *jingtou*
Head gardener: *yuantou*
Usher: *zhaoke*

East Offices
Provost: *dujian*
Prior: *jianyuan*
Subprior: *fusi*
Supervisory clerk: *kusi*
Rent collector: *jianshou*
Village agent: *yuanzhu*
Head miller: *niantou*
Head of wandering monks' hall: *liaoyuan*

Senior verger: *dianzhu*
Bell ringer: *zhongtou*
Drummer: *gutou*
Night patrol: *yexun*

West Rank
Head rector: *zuoyuan*
Rector: *shouzuo*
Senior instructor: *xitang*
Associate instructor: *houtang*
Assistant instructor: *tangzhu*
Secretary: *shuji*
Librarian: *zangzhu*
Proctor: *sengzhi*
Canon prefect: *zhizang*

Guest prefect: *zhike*
Meditation monk: *chantou*
Water-bearer: *sishui*

East Rank
Precentor: *weinuo*
Succentor: *yuezhong*
Deacon: *zushi*
Thurifer: *shaoxiang*
Record-keeper: *jilu*
Sacristan: *yibo*
Dispenser of medicine: *tangyao*
Attendant, acolyte: *shizhe*
Monks without formal positions, such as meditation monks: *qingzhong*
 "Pure guest": *qingke*
Travelling monk: *xingzhe*
Verger: *xiangdeng*

Chinese-Pinyin Glossary

ācārya 阿闍梨
ban 班
banshou 班首
Baohua Shan 宝华山
changzhu 常住
chantang 禅堂
chantou 禅头
chujia 出家
dangjia seng, dangjia shi 当家僧, 当家师
daochang 道场
dianzhu 殿主
dianzuo 典座
douguan 都管
dousi 都寺
dujian 都监
dusi 都司
fangtou 房头
fangzhang 方丈
fangzhang shi 方丈室
fantou 饭头
fashi 法师
fu jianyuan 副监院
fusi 副寺
guadan 挂单
gutou 鼓头
houtang 后堂

The Rambling Story of a Dream

huazhu 化主
Huiju si 慧居寺
jianshou 监收
jianyuan, jiansi 监院, 监寺
jiaoshou shi 教授师
jiemo shi 羯磨師
jietan 戒坛
jilu 记录
kufang 库房
fangtou 房头
kusi 库司
liaoyuan, liaozhu 寮院, 寮主
Longchang si 隆昌寺
Miaofeng Fudeng 妙峰福登
nei / wai zhishi 内 / 外 職事
neiqin 内勤
niantou 碾头
Qianhua Temple 千华寺
qingzhong 清众
ruyi liao 如意寮
senglusi 僧錄司
sengzhi 僧值
sengzhi, jiucha 僧知, 纠察
shanzhishi 善知识
shaoxiang 烧香
shizhe 侍者
shouzuo 首座
shuji 书记
siku 司库
sishui 司水
suixi 随喜
tang 堂

tangyao 汤药
tangzhu 堂主
tie'an 贴案
tongjie lu 同戒录
weina, karmadāna 维那
xiangban 香板
xiangdengshi 香灯师
xingtang 行堂
xingzhe 行者
xitang 西堂
yexun 夜巡
yibo, yibo shi 衣钵, 衣钵师
yinli shi 引礼师
yuezhong 悦众
yunshui 云水
zangzhu 藏主
zhibin 知宾
zhike 知客
zhishi 知事
zhishi 执事
zhisui 值岁
zhizang 知藏
zhongbantang 钟板堂
zhongtou 钟头
zhuangzhu 莊主
zuoyuan 座元
zushi 祖师

Bibliography

Chantang faqi yu guiju xiangjie. In *Fodizi wenku.* (9 October 2019). http://fodizi.net//fojiaozhishi/23082.html

Cheng, Anne. "Is Zhongguo the Middle Kingdom or Madhyadeśa?" In *OpenEdition Books*, Collège de France, 2020, books.openedition.org/cdf/7526?lang=en. Accessed 18 Mar. 2024.

Duti, Jianyue. *Santan chuanjie zhengfan.* CBETA Chinese Electronic Tripitaka Collection https://buddhism.lib.ntu.edu.tw/FULLTEXT/sutra/10thousand/X60n1128.pdf

Duti, Jianyue (*Jianyue laoren*). *Yimeng manyan.* Beijing: *Tuan jie chuban she*, 2018.

Duti, Jianyue (*Jianyue laoren*). *Yimeng manyan.* Hong Kong: Hong Kong Buddhist Printing Limited, 1994.

Duti, Jianyue (*Jianyue laoren*). *Yimeng manyan* (Ming). In *Jingdian wenxue wang.* (26 May 2020). https://www.now818.com/post/11371.html.

Eichman, Jennifer. "Humanizing the Study of Late Ming Buddhism." In Chung-Hwa Buddhist Journal (2013, 26: 153–185). New Taipei: Chung-Hwa Institute of Buddhist Studies. https://www.chibs.edu.tw/ch_html/chbj/26/6_Eichman(153-185).pdf

Fo shuo yulanpenjing shu xiaoheng chao. In *Huaren fojiao.* https://www.hrfjw.com/fojing/yulanpenjing/82537.html

Grant, Beata. *Eminent Nuns: Women Chan Masters of Seventeenth-Century China.* Honolulu: University of Hawai'i Press, 2009. https://terebess.hu/zen /Eminent-Nuns.pdf

"Guxiu wushisan can tuce." In *The Palace Museum.* (14 June 2023). https://www.dpm.org.cn/collection/embroider/229672

Heirman, Ann. "Shoes in Buddhist Monasteries from India to China: From Practical Attire to Symbol," *Acta Orientalia Academiae Scientiarum Hungaricae* 69, no. 4 (2016): 411–39. http://www.jstor.org/stable/26424896.

Hsieh, Ding-hwa. "Buddhist Nuns in Sung China (960–1279)." In *Journal of Song-Yuan Studies*, no. 30 (2000): 63–96. http://www.jstor.org/stable/23495823

Hucker, Charles O. *A Dictionary of Official Titles in Imperial China*. Taiwan ed. Taipei: Southern Materials Center, 1986.

Lepneva, Mariia. "Who Can Revive Buddhist Ordinations? Explaining the Eminence of Guxin Ruxin in Late Ming China." In *Religions* 13, no. 9: 844. (13 September 2022). https://doi.org/10.3390/rel13090844

Liu, Mingfang. *Baohua shan zhi*. 1784. Accessed on Internet Archive (27 June 2024). Contributed by: Cheng Yu Tung East Asian Library (University of Toronto), p. 43. https://ia902906.us.archive.org/4/items/baohuashanzhi01lium/baohuashanzhi01lium.pdf

Meinheit, Susan. *A newly acquired Tibetan Kanjur: The dragon tripitaka: 4 corners of the world*. In *Library of Congress Blogs*. Posted by Hoh, Anchi. (8 July 2016). https://blogs.loc.gov/international-collections/2016/07/a-newly-acquired-tibetan-kanjur-the-dragon-tripitaka/

Nienhauser, William H., Jr. "An Allegorical Reading of Han Yü's *Mao-Ying Chuan*" (Biography of Fur Point). In *Oriens Extremus*, Vol. 23, No. 2 (1976), pp. 153–174. https://www.jstor.org/stable/43382488

Orsborn, Matthew. "Śrāvaka Ordination in a Mahāyāna Embrace: Triple Platform Ordination in Chinese Buddhism." In *Pacific World*: 129–171. (20 September 2021). https://www.shin-ibs.edu/documents/pwj4/2/4-2-12-Orsborn.pdf

Prip-Møller, Johannes. *Chinese Buddhist Monasteries: Their Plan and Its Function as a Setting for Buddhist Monastic Life* [2d ed.]. Hong Kong: Hong Kong University Press, 1967.

Bibliography

(Master) Ranmiao. "*Dui chujiaren de chenghu ni zhidao duoshao?*" In *Xin lang foxue*. (19 June 2018). https://fo.sina.cn/intro/2018-06-19/detail-iheauxvy6097163.d.html

Shi, Kuanguang. "Wutai Shan During the Ming Dynasty." PhD diss., University of London, 2010. https://eprints.soas.ac.uk/33749/1/11010522.pdf

"*Shi zhong jingangxin*." In the *Fanwangjing* (Fascicle I). (1 August 2014). http://fodizi.net/qt/qita/14778.html

Shuyu, Yijie (1645–1721). *Dual Saṅgha ordination rites*. National Taiwan University. Accessed 18 August 2023. https://buddhism.lib.ntu.edu.tw/FULLTEXT/JR-AN/an594992.pdf

Terebess, Gábor (comp.). "Glossary of Zen Terms." https://terebess.hu/zen/szoto/szotar/szotar.html

Ṭhānissaro Bhikkhu. "Ordination." In *The Buddhist Monastic Code* (Vols. I & II). (Revised 1 July 2022). https://www.dhammatalks.org/vinaya/bmc/Section0054.html/

Wang, Hsuan-Li. "Gushan: The Formation of a Chan Lineage during the Seventeenth Century and Its Spread to Taiwan." PhD diss., Columbia University, 2014.

Welch, Holmes. *The Practice of Chinese Buddhism, 1900–1950*. Cambridge: Harvard University Press, 1973. https://terebess.hu/zen/mesterek/Holmes-Welch-The-Practice.pdf

Wen, Jinyü. *Jianyue laoren sixiang yanjiu*. In *Fojiao daohang*. (12 April 2009). https://www.fjdh.cn/wumin/2009/04/07210350873.html

Wen, Jinyü. *Lüzong qianhuapai famai*. In *Wuliang xiangguang*. http://fowap.goodweb.net.cn/news/news_view.asp?newsid=56351

Zurndorfer, Harriet T. "Violence and Political Protest in Ming and Qing China: Review and Commentary on Recent Research." In *International Review of Social History*, Vol. 28, No. 3 (1983), pp. 304–319. https://www.jstor.org/stable/44583728

About the translator: Lynne Mallinson (MA/Chinese Language and Literature; BA/Chinese, Math) is an independent scholar currently living in Oregon. She spent a number of fruitful years working and studying in Europe and the UK and completed intensive studies in classical Chinese linguistics and literature, history, philosophy, and art in Harbin and Taipei. She is a teacher, private tutor, writer, translator, editor, and artist.

eetc.xialiang@gmail.com

www.ingramcontent.com/pod-product-compliance
Lightning Source LLC
LaVergne TN
LVHW041759060526
838201LV00046B/1049